CCRP Publication Series

This is a continuation in the series of publications produced by the Center for Advanced Concepts and Technology (ACT), which was created as a "skunk works" with funding provided by the CCRP under the auspices of the Assistant Secretary of Defense (C3I). This program has demonstrated the importance of having a research program focused on the national security implications of the Information Age. It develops the theoretical foundations to provide DoD with information superiority and highlights the importance of active outreach and dissemination initiatives designed to acquaint senior military personnel and civilians with these emerging issues. The CCRP Publication Series is a key element of this effort.

Check our Web site for the latest CCRP activities and publications.

www.dodccrp.org

DoD Command and Control Research Program

ASSISTANT SECRETARY OF DEFENSE (C3I)
&
CHIEF INFORMATION OFFICER

Mr. John P. Stenbit

PRINCIPAL DEPUTY ASSISTANT SECRETARY OF DEFENSE (C3I)

Dr. Linton Wells, II

SPECIAL ASSISTANT TO THE ASD(C3I)
&
DIRECTOR, RESEARCH AND STRATEGIC PLANNING

Dr. David S. Alberts

Library of Congress Cataloging-in-Publication Data

Information age transformation: getting to a 21st century military / David S. Alberts.
   p. cm.
  Includes bibliographical references and index.
  ISBN 1-893723-06-2 (pbk.)
   1. Electronics in military engineering--United States. 2. Information technology.
I. Alberts, David S. (David Stephen), 1942-
UG485 .A42 1996
358--dc20

               96-14441

First printing, April 1996
Second printing, October 1996
Revision, June 2002

INFORMATION AGE
TRANSFORMATION

GETTING TO A
21ST CENTURY MILITARY

DAVID S. ALBERTS

Table of Contents

List of Figures

Acknowledgments

Many individuals have contributed to the development of the ideas contained in this book and helped in this undertaking. The research which ultimately formed the basis for the original manuscript was suggested by Vice Admiral Cebrowski (Ret.) when he was the J6. This updated and expanded version was supported by him in his current role as Director, Force Transformation. This book could not have been written without the active support provided to me by the senior leadership at OASD(C3I). To the current and recent Assistant Secretaries of Defense (C3I), Mr. John Stenbit, Dr. Linton Wells, II, and Mr. Arthur Money, I owe many thanks for the opportunity they have given me to be a part of the transformation of the DoD. In the years since the *Unintended Consequences of Information Age Technologies* was written, I have written or contributed to a number of other publications dealing with Information Age warfare. Working with me on many of these books and DoD reports and publications has been Mr. John Garstka, Dr. Richard Hayes, and Dr. David Signori. They, among others, have been involved in the development of many of the ideas expressed herein and have been active in their dissemination. Dr. Hayes has also worked with me to sharpen my arguments and clarify my thoughts.

I would also like to thank Ms. Priscilla Guthrie, Dr. Margaret Myers, and Mr. Owen Wormser, who took time from their hectic schedules to provide very helpful comments and suggestions. A lot of effort was involved in turning my manuscript into a CCRP publication. I owe a huge debt to Joseph Lewis and Alison Leary for editing this document, Margita Rushing for orchestrating the process and designing the layout, and to Bernie Pineau for designing the cover and making the graphics convey the intended message.

Preface

Transformation is a process of renewal, an adaptation to environment. Its pace and progress depend on the nature of the entity being transformed, its environment, and the drivers of the transformation. The object of a transformation may be an individual, a small organization, a large institution, an industry, a group of related entities, or even an entire society. Important aspects of the environment relate to the continued viability of the entity and the constraints on its ability to adapt. Change and human adaptation are always the essential ingredients in transformation. Change provides the stimulus needed to overcome the inertia associated with the status quo, "old" equilibrium, which was reached to accommodate a set of conditions that no longer apply. Transformations may or may not be managed. In fact, the degree to which a transformation of a large institution can be managed is a central question.

The national security environment and the nature of threats and challenges have been evolving since the collapse of the Soviet Union. The relative importance of a spectrum of traditional and nontraditional threats and the urgency of dealing with emerging threats have been vigorously debated. Recently, the DoD has moved from a threat-based strategy to a capabilities-based strategy and the debate has shifted accordingly. The events of September 11, 2001, have focused increasing attention on the need to transform the Department's organization from one finely-tuned for accomplishing traditional military missions to one that is capable of deterring, preventing, and if necessary, defeating a diverse set of nontraditional adversaries.

The enormity of the changes that we have experienced in the geopolitical and national security environments are equaled, if not exceeded, by the changes brought about by the advances in technology associated with the Information Age. Much has been written[1] about the impacts of information and telecommunications technologies on individuals, organizations, and societies. A profound connection exists among the capabilities associated with the Information Age, the geopolitical landscape, and national security.

This book is the first in a new series of CCRP books that will focus on the Information Age transformation of the Department of Defense. Accordingly, it deals with the issues associated with a very large governmental institution, a set of formidable impediments, both internal and external, and the nature of the changes being brought about by Information Age concepts and technologies. This book is not intended to deal with all of the issues associated with the DoD's adaptation to meet 21st-century challenges. Rather, it focuses its attention on the key dimension of change associated with Information Age technology—the quality and distribution of information within the organization—its richness, its reach, and the quality of the interactions.[2]

In 1995, I began work on a book entitled the *Unintended Consequences of Information Age Technologies*.[3] The first printing "sold out," and within 6 months a second, larger printing was made and has, subsequently, sold out as well. Over the years the ideas discussed in the book about the nature of future missions, freeing information from the chain of command, mission capability packages, and the need for their coevolution have taken root. They now are part and parcel of the emerging strategy for DoD transformation. With the acceptance of these ideas, interest in this book has been revived. In reviewing the manuscript with an eye towards a third printing, I came to the conclusion that it needed updating and started to edit the manuscript. As I became more and more immersed in the book, I realized that I had two choices. The first was to simply update the book, putting it into current language and context so that it could provide some background for those engaged in transformation. The second was to use the original book as the kernel for a new one, transporting, modifying, and adding text to incorporate ideas that have been developing since the book's initial publication. I have chosen the second approach in the hopes that it will provide a better point of departure for the urgent task of transforming the DoD to meet the challenges ahead. I have also tried to keep the book short and succinct to serve as an introduction rather than a comprehensive treatment of the subject. Thus, this new book supercedes the now out-of-print 1995 manuscript, which will now provide historical context for the development of these ideas.

---

[1]As a point of departure, please see: Alberts, David S. and Daniel S. Papp, eds., *Information Age Anthology*. Washington, DC: National Defense University and CCRP. June 1997-March 2001. Vols 1-3.

[2]This concept and its origins are discussed more fully in: Alberts, David S., John J. Gartska, Richard E. Hayes, and David A. Signori. *Understanding Information Age Warfare*. Washington, DC: CCRP. August 2001. p. 46.

[3]Alberts, David S. *The Unintended Consequences of Information Age Technologies: Avoiding the Pitfalls, Seizing the Initiative*. Washington, DC: National Defense University. April 1996.

CHAPTER 1

Introduction

M ilitary organizations are, by their very nature, resistant to change. This is in no small part due to the fact that the cost of error is exceedingly high. Change, particularly change that may affect the relationships among organizations and between commanders and their subordinates, presents significant risks and therefore generates considerable concern. The explosion of information technologies has set in motion a virtual tidal wave of change that is in the process of profoundly affecting both organizations and individuals in multiple dimensions. The military is no exception. At the very beginning of the Information Age, technological advances made it possible to provide more complete, more accurate, and more timely information to decisionmakers. As the costs of processing and communications power tumbled, it became cost-effective for organizations to adopt and utilize information technologies in more and more situations.

Information and Military Organizations

Military organizations have traditionally provided information to forces in three ways:

1. Commands (directives and guidance);

2. Intelligence (information about the adversary and the environment); and

3. Doctrine (how you are going to do it).

Commands serve to define the specific task at hand. Intelligence provides information about the environment in which the task is to be carried out. Doctrine provides the rules of the game or standard operating procedures. Doctrine, unlike commands and intelligence, is not provided in real-time, but serves to shape the culture and mindsets of the individuals involved. Thus, information has, until recently, been inseparable from commanders, command structures, and command systems.

Each of these three ways of communicating information about what is expected of subordinate organizations and individuals has evolved over time to be mutually supportive of an overall command concept or approach matched to the nature of the conflict and the capabilities of the forces. The success of military operations depends to a large extent upon the ability to coordinate activities to achieve synchronized effects.[1] Ensuring that individuals behave as intended or as expected in the face of uncertainty (the fog of war) and under stress is a key to achieving coordinated activities. The selective dissemination of information has traditionally been used as a tool to define and shape the environment in which soldiers operate and to ensure conforming behavior.

The military is now on the road to becoming an Information Age organization. This book explores what this means in terms of the nature of the information that will be available to participants in a mission, how this information is disseminated, how it is used, and the implications for command and control, organization, and doctrine. This Information Age transformation is fraught with risks as well as opportunities. Both are a direct consequence of the changes in the nature of available information, its pattern of dissemination, and the resultant organizational adaptation.

Organization of this Book

This book begins by noting contemporary thinking and vocabulary as embodied in recent DoD publications, and moves on to provide context for the discussion of an Information Age transformation of DoD. This contemporary thinking is juxtaposed with the lingering questions that stimulated the original version of this book. The result is a book that highlights the historic tension between risks and opportunities. To set the stage for the discussion about the nature of the DoD's Information Age transformation, a set of *Reflections* is offered in the Chapter 3. This section contains an assessment of where we are now (Taking Stock), the nature of the effort that will be involved (Engineering vs. Innovation), and what this transformation is really all about (Transformation and Value).

A set of observations about the nature of change and the challenges in dealing with change follows. The case is made for an aggressive approach, one that is not constrained by current notions and practices and one that is not overly preoccupied with avoiding pitfalls.

The examination of the nature of an Information Age transformation begins with a review of the impact that information technologies are having or could have on the warfighter. This discussion extends into a consideration of the nature of future warfare and the characteristics of an Information Age military.

The identification of concerns related to the introduction of information technologies and the identification of a set of remedies to address the causes of these concerns provides the basis for the articulation of a prudent and effective strategy for effecting an Information Age transformation. This strategy for transformation is built around experimentation with network-centric concepts designed to leverage the power of Information Age technologies and the coevolution of mission capability packages, a process designed to minimize the risks and seize the opportunities associated with the application of these technologies to military operations. The iterative and inclusive nature of a process of coevolution helps to expose and deal with the kinds of disconnects that are the root cause of the adverse consequences that have been associated with insertions of information technologies. As a result, risks are reduced and the ability to recognize and take advantage of opportunities is increased.

This discussion is followed by a proposed strategy for transformation, one that is believed to address the issues associated with anticipated and unanticipated, intended and unintended consequences. Next is an examination of how to measure progress toward transformation and assess the value associated with this progress. Some of the key characteristics associated with transformation, suggested milestones along the way, and metrics that are related to progress and value are provided for the reader's consideration.

The next section discusses what is required in a Transformation Roadmap. A section that identifies critical research areas that are not receiving adequate attention follows.

The book concludes with the thought that while adverse unintended consequences are an inevitable by-product of transformation, this fact should not deter us from encouraging and embracing change.

---

[1]The original text was *synchronized operations*. The change to *effects* recognizes the work that has been done since 1995 on effects-based operations. The CCRP is preparing to release a book on EBO by Dr. Edward A. Smith: *From Network-Centric to Effects-Based Operations*.

CHAPTER 2

Background and Purpose

DoD is fully committed to taking advantage of Information Age concepts and technologies.[1][2] *Joint Vision 2010* and *2020* specifically focus on the power of information as an enabler of combat power. Network Centric Warfare[3] (NCW) translates these broad vision statements into a way ahead. NCW is a set of warfighting concepts[4] designed to create and leverage information. Network Centric Warfare is, as the opening line of the *NCW Report to the Congress* states, "no less than the embodiment of an Information Age transformation of the DoD."[5] NCW has been called "the emerging theory of war" and is, in any number of its various manifestations, being adopted by organizations throughout the DoD. NCW is the organizing principle that guides the military's adoption of information technologies and its adaptation to these technologies.

The tenets of NCW are:[6]

1. A robustly networked force improves information sharing.

2. Information sharing and collaboration enhance the quality of information and shared situational awareness.

3. Shared situational awareness enables self-synchronization.

4. These, in turn, dramatically increase mission effectiveness.

Thus, NCW involves both:

• The provision of vastly increased access to information at all echelons, and

• A redefinition of the relationships among participants in a mission and between commanders and subordinates.

The full implications and consequences of achieving a robustly networked force and of adopting network-centric concepts of operation will, of course, not be clear for years to come.

The analysis that formed the kernel of this book was initiated in 1995 as a result of concerns expressed by the Chairman of the Joint Chiefs of Staff[7] regarding the unintended consequences of providing broader and deeper access to information. Implicit in those concerns are uncertainties about the impact of separating information flows from the command structure and the effects of almost unlimited amounts of information upon decisionmaking. Questions were raised regarding exactly how much information should be provided to each echelon. It is interesting to note that this question (articulated in 1995) assumes a "push" paradigm that is now out of step[8] with current thinking about information dissemination.

The appropriate command concepts for a robustly networked force and an information-rich battlefield have, as yet, not been fully determined, nor will they be for some time to come. Concerns have been raised regarding the potential adverse effects of increased visibility into operations at all levels, including the increased potential for information overload, second guessing, micro-management, stifling of initiatives, and distraction.

A separate but related set of concerns involves the manner in which our potential adversaries adopt and utilize Information Age technologies and the capabilities that result. A final set of concerns involves our ability to protect information and information assets for our own use and to deny our enemies the same advantage and to deal with failures of and degradations in the systems that provide information to decisionmakers, shooters, and others with crucial roles. There has been a tendency to focus on the commander as the sole decisionmaker in both command and control analyses and in developing requirements for command and control systems. NCW inherently involves decisions taken across the battlespace in support of command intent, where decisions are characterized by a greater degree of freedom than is normally associated with a traditional approach to command and control. Therefore, it is now recognized that there are many decisionmakers in the battlespace that need to be explicitly considered in order to understand the behavior of the force.

The purpose of this book is to articulate a strategy for introducing and using Information Age technologies that accomplishes two things:

1. The identification and avoidance of adverse unintended consequences; and

2. The ability to recognize and capitalize on unexpected opportunities.

The DoD's experimentation with information technologies and NCW concepts has shown that both pitfalls and opportunities are present. Experience to date with emerging technologies and experience in applying the principles of NCW highlight the need and the importance of being able to rapidly and systematically identify and avoid pitfalls, seize opportunities that result from vastly improved information, and the ability to get it to the right people, at the right times, in the right forms.[9]

Given that potential adversaries have access to virtually the same information and information technologies that we have,[10] the margin for victory will be determined by our success in effecting DoD's Information Age transformation. Our ability to integrate a wide variety of systems into a true system of systems[11] will depend not only upon our technical skills, but also upon how well we adapt our processes, doctrine, organizations, and culture to take advantage of the opportunities that technology affords. Our success will depend not upon our technical prowess, but on our ability to adapt and leverage the capabilities provided by technology.

This book addresses not only the nature of the adaptation that is thought to be required, but also the process of transformation itself. Transformation is not an endstate, but a process; a process that is driven by changes in environment (threats and opportunities), fueled by innovation, and paced by institutional and cultural constraints. Transformation is not about something that will happen sometime in the future (beyond the Five-Year Defense Program). Transformation can and should be about what we do now and in the future. There is much we can do with the means at our disposal if we can change our mindsets, attitudes, and relationships. As time goes by, more and more variables will become controllable and we will have more means to apply to the task of transformation. Nevertheless, we all need to begin by facing the first step, thinking about what transformation really means and how we can advance the cause today, tomorrow, and beyond. The aim is to help prepare us for the journey ahead.

---

[1]"Message of the Secretary of Defense." *Annual Report to the President and the Congress*. Defense Secretary William S. Cohen. 2001.

[2]*Network Centric Warfare Department of Defense Report to Congress*. July 2001. p. 2-1.

[3]Alberts, David S., John J. Garstka, and Frederick P. Stein. *Network Centric Warfare: Developing and Leveraging Information Superiority*. Washington, DC: CCRP. August 1999. p. 2.

[4]Although expressed in warfighting terms, the basic concepts of NCW apply more broadly to all manners of military operations. The term *network-centric operations* has been used in this regard.

[5]*Network Centric Warfare Department of Defense Report to Congress*. July 2001. p. i.

[6]*Ibid*. p. i.

[7]The Chairman of the Joint Chiefs of Staff at the time was General John Shalikashvili.

[8]It is now widely accepted that a "pull" paradigm is more appropriate for reasons that are discussed later in this book.

[9]Information Superiority has many definitions. A popular one is "getting the right information to the right people, at the right times, and in the right forms, while denying adversaries the ability to do the same." This has been taken by some to imply (mistakenly) a push orientation. It is an end to be sought.

[10]During the operations in Afghanistan, there was concern that commercial imagery of the AOR would compromise U.S. Forces and operations. This imagery was kept out of adversary hands by an arrangement that provided the DoD with exclusive rights to this imagery. While this stopgap measure may have worked in this case, it is certain that in the future, more and more information will flow to potential adversaries.

[11]I prefer the term *federation of systems*. See: Krygiel, Annette J. *Behind the Wizard's Curtain: An Integration Environment for a System of Systems*. Washington, DC: CCRP. July 1999. p. 40.

CHAPTER 3

Reflections

S ince 1995, many of the ideas contained in the *Unintended Consequences of Information Age Technologies* have taken root or at least have been widely discussed. The current leadership of DoD has done much to signal their interest and commitment to transformation. The need for vastly increased information sharing and collaboration is being recognized. The need to move (and move quickly) to a "post before use" paradigm and from a push- to a pull-oriented approach to information access has become a top priority of this administration. Indeed, the need for a secure, robust, and interoperable infostructure to support NCW and the transformation of our business processes is increasingly accepted.

As evidence of this growing recognition of the importance of information to emerging warfighting concepts and capabilities, the recent budgets reflect a significantly increased emphasis on C4ISR capabilities. Experimentation activities are beginning to move beyond an exercise mentality. NCW proofs of concept are beginning to accumulate and convince even some of the diehard skeptics. The war on terrorism has added a sense of urgency and lowered barriers to innovation. Experiences in Bosnia, Kosovo, and Afghanistan have provided real-world laboratories where important learning and proofs of concepts have occurred.

Taking Stock

Despite this demonstrable progress, there is much more that needs to be done to prepare DoD for the changes that will come. A lack of understanding of what transformation really means remains fairly widespread. All too often, transformation is confused with modernization. All too often, transformation efforts are inwardly focused. Organizations claim that they can transform themselves in isolation. The focus is on how we operate rather than on how we can work with others to create opportunities for synergy. The recognition that transformation is inherently joint and coalition has not yet reached critical mass. In the Information Age, jointness is not an applique but an inherent property of everything we do. In many quarters, there is still much resistance to sharing information, to increasing the reach of collaboration, and to greater integration.

Unfortunately, innovation is currently stifled as much as it is rewarded. This needs to change. A look at the talent that leaves the military because of a perceived (and often real) lack of opportunity needs to be undertaken. Corrective measures to address this brain drain need to be expedited. Promotions based upon old core competencies do not provide the DoD with the talent it needs in the Information Age. Moreover, it discourages those with the talents the DoD needs.

In the wake of September 11th, there has been a renewed sense of national pride and a desire to serve. If we are to capitalize upon this opportunity to tap a new pool of talent, we need to address the above and other personnel-related issues (education, training, role redefinition, etc.) promptly. Being part of an historic transformation is a rare and rewarding opportunity. We need to make sure that it is this reality that our brave and dedicated men and women experience rather than frustrating bouts with entrenched bureaucrats.

Many DoD processes are consensual by custom. Disruptive innovation and consensual change are not often compatible. When it comes to any significant change, there will be groups of advocates, early adopters, late adopters, and resisters to the end. Unpleasant as it is, leadership needs to root out the resisters and prod the late adopters, while supporting and protecting the advocates and early adopters.

It has been often been pointed out that peacetime militaries and wartime militaries behave very differently. Increasingly, the types of warfare that we are experiencing and can expect in the future blur the distinctions between war and peace. Since September 11th, we have been at war. We need to make this realization widespread and tie transformation to our success in this war effort.

Engineering vs. Innovation

Increasingly, I see evidence of a belief by some that we can engineer everything, even innovation, which is heavily cultural. Engineering involves the "application of scientific principles to practical ends."[1] Hence, engineering is an applied science. The basic assumption is that there is a body of laws, knowledge, experience, and tools that the engineer can apply. Innovation is something "new and unusual."[2] Thus there is, as yet, no established body of knowledge, laws, or experience to apply. Yet there are many who still approach innovation in the same way that they would engineer a system. The result is, at best, incremental improvements that fail to fully realize the potential of Information Age technologies.

Our requirements processes have this engineering flavor. They assume we know what the requirements are and can state them with the necessary precision needed for an engineered solution.[3] There is still a very important role for engineering in the transformation. This role is to turn the system capabilities called for in a coevolved military capability package concept into a fielded reality. The focus of our engineering talents needs to be directed to the development of prototyping environments and ways to turn engineering prototypes into operational prototypes, and then into products.

Even on their home turf (systems), engineers will increasingly be up against the limits of their art and their practice. This is because, in a robustly networked world, the environments in which systems need to operate are more and more outside of the control of any organization and its engineers. "Systems of systems" is a description of this reality. However, some have understood this to mean that we can engineer a system of systems. This is not the reality of the Information Age. The collection of systems we use to accomplish our tasks are far from a neatly engineered system of systems, rather they are a federation of systems. That is, we are really looking at a collection of systems where individual systems have equal, peer-to-peer relationships with one another, but are united for mutual benefit.

Engineers are not the only ones who like and demand specifications upfront. Almost everyone in the long list of decisionmakers that are involved in creating and managing a DoD activity or program wants to know, with far more precision than is possible, what they are buying, approving, managing, and testing. They have been raised to focus on the product. It is difficult for people whose entire careers have been centered around the specification of a product to refocus their attention instead on the process that produces the product. However, this change in perspective is key to DoD transformation. Instead of investing in a long list of products (programs), the DoD must reorient mindsets and existing processes to focus on the people and the processes that can and will produce transformational capabilities.

Transformation and Value

The move from the Industrial Age to the Information Age has changed the relative values associated with the sources of wealth: land, labor, and capital. In the Information Age, land has relatively less value[4] than it did before, continuing a trend that began with the transition from an agrarian to an industrial society. The value of labor has remained high, but it is a different kind of labor that is in demand. Physical labor has been greatly devalued, but the value of intellectual labor, or what we call intellectual capital, has greatly increased. The relative value of capital has, like land, been diminished because it now requires less capital to enter into Information Age markets, develop information-related products, and distribute them. In many ways, the Information Age has brought equal opportunity to the marketplace by lowering the previously high barriers to entry that resulted from the need to have enough land and capital to make a venture successful. Not only have cost-related barriers been lowered, but geographic barriers as well. One can now participate in, for example, the software sector of the economy from literally anywhere on earth.

It stands to reason that the values associated with the military equivalents of land, labor, and capital are also in flux. Hence, the Information Age has not only affected the relative importance of the sources of wealth, changing the dynamics of wealth creation and maintenance, but it has also altered the relative importance of the sources of combat power.

The move to Network Centric Warfare, the military embodiment of Information Age concepts and technologies, is redefining the basic sources of combat power, enhancing the value of some things, and devaluing others. Maneuver, mass, surprise, firepower, and logistics have for centuries been the coins of the military realm. Surprise remains a key asset. But in the Information Age, information is transforming both the concepts of mass and maneuver, redefining firepower, and greatly simplifying logistics. Information can, in effect, be directly substituted in the "manufacture" of each of these capabilities.

The massing of forces is being transformed into a massing of effects (without the physical movement). Maneuver is less and less about being able to get a sizable amount of men and material somewhere in a hurry and more and more about either being pre-positioned correctly or about being able to have small groups move successfully on a nonlinear battlefield. The mass previously associated with firepower is being increasingly replaced with precision, made possible by information. Logistics has been greatly simplified by the de-massing of the force and by increasingly current and complete information.

Just as the dramatically changed relative values of land, labor, and capital have affected business models and organizations and the values they place on various corporate capabilities, NCW is changing the values associated with DoD investment choices. Some capabilities (and the processes and assets associated with these capabilities) are increasing in relative value while other aspects of a mission capability package are decreasing in relative value.

These changes are all about the marginal return on investment (ROI). For example, given that the DoD has a certain mix of assets in the inventory, what future investment strategy will result in the greatest overall return? In the Information Age, the answer (with increasing frequency) is increased investment in information-related capabilities. Depending on the situation, this investment could be in collecting, processing, displaying, or disseminating, or any combination of these.

A critic might ask, "Given that information has always been important in warfare, why suddenly does it make sense to invest relatively more in information than other military assets?" The answer is very simple. The Information Age has changed the economics of information, making it far less expensive to attain greater richness and reach for a given investment. This change in the economics of information makes it relatively cheaper than platforms or personnel. This, in turn, then makes the ROI for a dollar spent on information greater than it was before.

But, it is imperative that we remember that an investment in information will not realize its potential value without corresponding changes in organization, doctrine, materiel, and approaches to command and control. The need to change the way we do business (to take advantage of the opportunities that Information Age technologies afford) is often given lip service, but all too often these necessary changes in other elements of the mission capability packages are strongly resisted in practice. The changes that are resisted the most are changes to command approach and organizational arrangements. These changes are the ones that have the most profound effects on ROI. The result is that the potential value of investments in information are not recognized and if they are, they are not fully realized.

Traditions die hard. It needs to be remembered that our traditional approach to organizations, doctrine, and command and control have evolved in the marketplace as a function of the economics of warfare. Now that the economics have changed, we need to let the marketplace, not tradition, dictate how we fight, command, organize, equip, and train. We need to judge traditions dispassionately. Not all traditions are worth keeping.

Thus, changes in the economics of warfare will result in a reordering of the returns on investment associated with different defense capabilities. The investment choices that are being devalued, as a result of the Information Age, include: non-networked, non-interoperable platforms, sensors, systems, command organizations, facilities, personal assets that represent high-value targets to an adversary,[5] massive lift capabilities, heavy units, traditional doctrine, exercises, traditional planning processes, the push paradigm, and some core competencies.

One could argue that the primary source of opposition to transformation comes from those organizations and individuals that find that their current capabilities are being devalued. They mistakenly think that they are being devalued. These individuals and organizations could increase their value by developing and adopting new capabilities and core competencies that are a better response to the emerging national security environment and that support the conduct of NCW.

Stand-alone platforms will become less and less important because the value of platforms in NCW is not determined by their ability to operate independently, but by their ability to operate as part of a team. Therefore, to stay relevant, today's platforms will need to become fully "net ready," sharing the information they collect with others, and self-synchronizing their actions with other network nodes based upon command[6] intent. Platforms will no longer belong to a particular organization, but be fully joint, with their assets being tasked collaboratively.

New platforms will need to be designed to be better adapted to the emerging threat environment. As today's platforms become vulnerable, high-value targets, tomorrow's platforms will need to be smaller, more stealthy, and less costly so that they can be proliferated in large numbers and usefully deployed in swarms.

Doctrine now significantly lags behind developments on the battlefield. Exploring new network-centric concepts with existing doctrine as a point of departure constrains the imagination. Why? Experiments and actual operations must be the source of emerging doctrine, not the recipients of its wisdom. Institutions whose bureaucratic raison d'être is to produce doctrine need to re-examine how they can best contribute to the transformation.

Everyone needs to take a fresh look at what they should consider to be their core competencies. Many will find that some of their traditional competencies are no longer as valuable as they once were and that they need to develop new competencies. In addition, everyone will need to master new competencies that are essential to Information Age organizations. These include sharing of information, quickly and efficiently pulling information from a federation of systems, collaboration, and self-synchronization.

---

[1]*Webster's II New Riverside Dictionary*. New York: Houghton Mifflin Company. 1996.
[2]*Ibid.*

[3]AFCEA Study Team. Evolutionary Acquisition Study. Fairfax, VA: AFCEA, June 7, 1993.

[4]The term *relatively less value* is easily misunderstood. It should not be taken to mean that land, as a commodity, is worth less than before in absolute terms. Rather this expression means that, as a determination of wealth, land has lost its relative *influence*, that is, it is less important than before as a source of wealth.

[5]Many have foreseen the day when no one will be able to afford to field high-value targets because they will be too difficult to conceal and defend given the proliferation of Information Age capabilities.

[6]NCW involves a shift in focus from the idea of commander's intent to a concept of command intent. This reflects the very notion of NCW and a recognition that today's missions are inherently coalition and so complex that the very sense of what the mission is all about is derived from more than any single individual, but rather the congruent intent of a variety of decisionmakers.

CHAPTER 4

Dealing with the Challenges of Change

There is always an upside and a downside to change. Often there is no real choice; an individual or organization must change to prosper or even to survive. Clearly, the first order of business is to recognize that change is needed. The second is to understand in broad terms the nature of the change that is required. Finally, there is the task of undertaking change.

For over a decade, there has been a fairly widespread recognition that DoD needs to change. But, of course, there has been a vigorous debate regarding the degree and nature of the change required. In recent years, there has been a growing recognition of the need to shift our focus from traditional combat to other parts of the mission spectrum. Also in recent years, the theory of NCW was developed, and in a relatively short time, has captured the imagination of many throughout the DoD and, indeed, the world. Thus, to some extent, the step of understanding the nature of the change required has been taken.

The DoD has begun, with joint and Service experimentation,[1] to take the third step. However, review of these activities[2][3] reveals that all too often, new information capabilities are examined with existing, minimally modified concepts of operation and processes, or at best paired with someone's a priori idea of the solution. What are not fully recognized or appreciated are the enormous gains that can be achieved through exploration and discovery of new ways of doing business, particularly if they are not constrained by tradition or prevailing wisdom. While the results of NCW-related experimentation to date have been impressive (100 percent or more increases in measures associated with combat power[4]), they barely scratch the surface of what is possible.

Some argue that the problems and risks associated with change (certainly change in something as time tested as command and control) can be addressed simply by avoiding significant changes. Others advocate that any changes should be introduced slowly and systematically, thoroughly testing proposed alterations until the probability of error is acceptably low. In many circumstances, these very conservative approaches may be appropriate. Given that our new adversaries have not remained static and are displaying a capacity to think asymmetrically with great innovation to circumvent our strengths and attack our weaknesses, a conservative approach to change will not adequately prepare us for the challenges ahead.

The events of September 11, 2001, have clearly focused attention on the need to deal with the full mission spectrum and have moved us from spirited debate to spirited action. These events demonstrated conclusively that, despite considerable investments over the years in collection and intelligence assets, we were not able to develop sufficient situation awareness. A part of the problem is that we need new kinds of collectors. But perhaps more importantly, we need a way to ensure that we bring a greater variety of expertise, experience, and perspective to the information that we have. Information technologies, most notably those related to information sharing, collaboration, and visualization enable the kinds of network-centric organizations that can improve our ability to bring all of our information and all of our knowledge and experience to bear. As we will face more and more situations that are unfamiliar to us, our ability to do this becomes more and more important.

Prior to September 11th, we seemed preoccupied with the risks associated with change. Since September 11th, there has been increased recognition that a failure to embrace change carries with it its own set of risks and that these risks are significant. Thus, we are faced with the task of balancing different kinds of risks.

Preoccupation with the problem of avoiding or mitigating any adverse unintended consequences inherent in the adoption of information technologies is as harmful as proceeding with a disregard for unintended consequences. Care must be taken to adopt an approach to transformational change that is enabling, rather than limiting. The DoD is not in a position to take the apparently safe and comfortable slow road to the introduction of change. The environment in which we must operate is being transformed in a number of critical dimensions. Consequently, business as usual (the default decision) carries with it significant adverse consequences of its own. Thus, doing little or nothing turns out to be neither conservative nor safe.

The low cost of obtaining Information Age technologies will help potential adversaries improve their military capabilities as they learn to leverage these technologies effectively. Thus, inaction will lead down a path that exposes us to new and improved adversary capabilities that we may not be able to counter effectively without changes of our own. In addition, a failure to take advantage of opportunities to improve cost effectiveness translates into less capability no matter what increases are likely in the defense budget.

The pace of the advances in information technologies and their adoption make it imperative that our approach to change must be capable of keeping pace or it is doomed to failure from the start. In addition, we must recognize that there are two kinds of risks associated with the selection of an approach to change. In addition to the widely recognized risks associated with adverse consequences, there are the risks associated with the failure to recognize and capitalize on unexpected opportunities to do things more effectively and efficiently. Thus, risk management becomes the name of the game because risk avoidance is not possible.

Since we cannot stop, slow down, or control the pace of innovation in the information domain or totally prevent the unintended consequences associated with these innovations, we must introduce and adapt to information technologies using a strategy that:

• Identifies and anticipates negative repercussions and enables us to avoid those repercussions or minimize their impacts;

- Recognizes and takes advantage of unexpected opportunities; and

- Balances the risks associated with the failure to achieve these two objectives.

This strategy must also be capable of facilitating change fast enough to keep pace with exogenous forces impacting technologies and technologies' adoption by potential adversaries.

A transformation strategy designed to fully leverage information and information technologies requires alterations in our concepts of operation, doctrine, organizations, and force structure. Associated changes in logistics, education, and training will also be required. Without the coevolution—meaning concurrent changes in each of these elements necessary to field a real capability—we will only obtain incremental[5] improvements in effectiveness and efficiency while foreclosing opportunities for the order of magnitude improvements necessary to maintain the winning edge.

---

[1]It should be noted that JFCOM's experimentation organization was only stood up 2 years ago.

[2]Alberts, David S., John J. Garstka, Richard E. Hayes, and David A. Signori. *Understanding Information Age Warfare*. Washington, DC: CCRP. August 2001. p. 285.

[3]*Network Centric Warfare Department of Defense Report to Congress*. July 2001. p. 7-1.

[4]*Network Centric Warfare Department of Defense Report to Congress*. July 2001. p. 8-1.

[5]Actually, in some cases organizations may become dysfunctional because a mismatch between the person best equipped to make a decision by virtue of information availability is not the person doctrinally vested with the authority.

CHAPTER 5

Information Technology Impacts on the Warfighter

Information technologies, for the purposes of this analysis, include collection, processing, display, and communications technologies. Processing technologies include data fusion and analysis, as well as support for decisionmaking and sensemaking, such as knowledge-based expert systems and systems that support cognition. Display technologies include visualization tools and techniques.

Advances in these technologies have resulted in an enormous amount of near real-time information being potentially available to individuals anywhere at anytime. The intelligence level of systems and our confidence in their ability has also increased dramatically to the point where life-and-death decisions are now routinely being made automatically by computers, albeit with varying degrees of human supervision.

Even at this early point in the Information Age, the battlefield is awash with vastly improved quality and increased amounts of information. The dynamics of information dissemination have changed considerably in the latter half of the 20th century, from flowing primarily through organizational hierarchies or command structures to the point where significant amounts of information are obtained outside of these vertical flows and increasingly from non-DoD sources. Thus, what was once predominantly a highly constrained and vertical information flow has evolved into a mix of vertical and horizontal flows that extends beyond the DoD.

And more, much more is still to come. Networking and wireless technologies have untethered us both organizationally and geographically. We are on the verge of "Internet 3.0,"[1] which incorporates a set of distributed capabilities (processing, storage, network services, and collaborative environments) that enable peer-to-peer (P2P) and dynamically reconfigurable small group interactions (collaborations).

The FY03 DoD Budget provides for a major increase in C4ISR-related capabilities that will, in about a decade when combined with progress in the private sector, effectively eliminate bandwidth as a constraint. As our ability to share information increases, each participant in a military mission will gain more and more access to information.

Solutions to dealing with today's information flows will not necessarily work with tomorrow's vastly increased flows. The amount, quality, and dynamics of information dissemination have already begun to impact the ways decisions are allocated (delegation) and the manner in which those decisions are made. NCW is all about changing decisionmaking processes and topologies. It involves moving from an Industrial

Age model, where information is collected at the edges and moved to the center for decisionmaking, to an Information Age model, where the edge is empowered to make decisions based upon command intent and high quality situation awareness. The effectiveness of an Industrial Age organization depends upon the decisionmaking ability of one person (or a small number of persons) at the center and the ability to parse and communicate decisions, in the form of guidance, to subordinates such that their actions are synchronized. Thus, centralized deliberate planning has been the traditional focus of command and control systems. Early in the Information Age, information technologies were employed to incrementally improve this traditional command and control process. With NCW, there has been a focus on replacing the traditional command model with a new one—one based upon self-synchronization enabled by shared awareness.[23]

Thus (as shown in Figure 1), advances in information technologies provide us with significant opportunities both to improve our ability to command and control our forces and to improve our force capabilities.

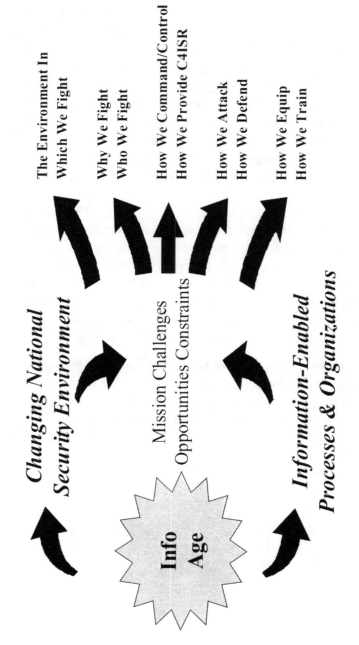

The Environment In
Which We Fight

Why We Fight
Who We Fight

How We Command/Control
How We Provide C4ISR

How We Attack
How We Defend

How We Equip
How We Train

Changing National
Security Environment

Mission Challenges
Opportunities Constraints

Information-Enabled
Processes & Organizations

Info
Age

Figure 1. The New Environment

Our information-related vulnerabilities have also increased. Increased reliance on high-tech systems for information collection, interpretation, processing, analysis, communication, and display has made failures in these systems more disruptive. The ubiquitous nature of these technologies provides our potential adversaries with capabilities that help them understand how to attack our information assets and give them the tools to do so. Our command and control systems can no longer be evaluated using measures of merit (MOMs) related solely to the production of quality information in a timely manner. It is now important to consider such attributes as availability, integrity, and authenticity of the information, its ease of use, and its value-added for decisionmaking.

Command and control has long been a recognized force multiplier,[4] and improvements in information technologies offer tremendous opportunities to perfect existing approaches and explore new ones. Quicker, better decisions will allow us to operate more effectively within the enemy's decision cycle, providing us with an opportunity to control engagements. This is referred to as the speed of command. Improvements in information technologies also enhance the capabilities of our weapons, providing them with increased standoff capability and accuracy. Experiences in Afghanistan have shown that when forces can interoperate in new and innovative ways, good things happen. The key battle of Mazar-e-Sharif was, in the words of the Secretary of Defense, a combination "of the ingenuity of the U.S. Special Forces, the most advanced, precision-guided munitions in the U.S. arsenal delivered by U.S. Navy,

Air Force, and Marine Corps crews, and the courage of valiant one-legged Afghan fighters on horseback."[5]

But the opportunities that new, improved, and interoperable weapons and command and control systems offer cannot be successfully exploited unless we rethink our concepts of operations and our approach to command and control, change processes, doctrine, and organizational structures, and provide the required personnel the education, training, and experiences they need. This theme was stressed in a speech that Secretary Rumsfeld gave to students at the National Defense University in which he said, "A revolution in military affairs is about more than building new high-tech weapons, though that is certainly part of it. It's also about new ways of thinking, and new ways of fighting."[6] Dealing with disruptive innovation[7][8] is, to many, a daunting prospect. But, as the remainder of this book will show, we have no alternative but to treat the adoption of new information-related capabilities holistically, that is, to consider them in a mission capability package context.

A major issue is the pace of change expressed, for example, by Moore's Law.[9] With new capabilities being available so quickly, how can we possibly learn to effectively use these capabilities before they, in turn, become obsolete? The answer lies in a transformation strategy that anticipates technology, rather than trails technology. This approach is concept-driven rather than technology-driven. We do not have to wait for improvements in technology to actually occur before considering new approaches to command and control, concepts of operation, doctrine, or organizational arrangements. Quite the contrary, if we wait, the inertia associated with developing and implementing these changes will keep us permanently behind the power curve. This does not imply that changes in command and control or force capabilities must necessarily precede alterations to concepts of operation or doctrine.

In reality, these elements (e.g., concept of operations, doctrine, technology, etc.) constitute a package that, taken as a whole, provides real operational capability that can be applied in a specific mission. A mission-specific perspective is important because no organizational structure or approach to command and control is going to be well-suited for the range of likely missions; missions as diverse as traditional major theater wars (MTWs), small-scale contingencies, counter-terrorism, and peace operations. New measures of merit (MOMs) will be required that must be mission-related. For example, classic measures, such as attrition or taking and holding territory, are not relevant in many mission contexts. In addition to the need to employ metrics that reflect success in nontraditional missions (e.g., normalcy indicators for OOTW), the very broad spectrum of missions that the military may be called upon to undertake and the uncertainties associated with them give rise to a need for metrics that reflect agility.[10]

---

[1]Fagin, Robert and Chris Kwak. *Internet Infrastructure and Services*. Bear Stearns, May 2001.
[2]Alberts, David S., John J. Garstka, and Frederick P. Stein. *Network Centric Warfare: Developing and Leveraging Information Superiority*. Washington, DC: CCRP. August 1999. pp. 6, 36, 66.

[3]Alberts, David S. *The Unintended Consequences of Information Age Technologies: Avoiding the Pitfalls, Seizing the Initiative.* Washington, DC: National Defense University. April 1996. p. 40.

[4]*Ibid.* p. 279.

[5]Jim Garamone. "Flexibility, Adaptability at Heart of Military Transformation." *American Forces Press Service.* Jan 31, 2002.

[6]CNN: http://www.cnn.com/2002/US/01/31/rumsfeld.speech/index.html. January 31, 2002.

[7]*Network Centric Warfare Department of Defense Report to Congress.* July 2001. pp. 12-14.

[8]Alberts, David S. *The Unintended Consequences of Information Age Technologies: Avoiding the Pitfalls, Seizing the Initiative.* Washington, DC: National Defense University. April 1996. pp. 63-4.

[9]The observation that the logic density of silicon integrated circuits has closely followed the curve (bits per square inch) = $2^{(t - 1962)}$ where t is time in years; that is, the amount of information storable on a given amount of silicon has roughly doubled every year since the technology was invented. This relation, first uttered in 1964 by semiconductor engineer Gordon Moore (who co-founded Intel 4 years later) held until the late 1970s, at which point the doubling period slowed to 18 months.

[10]See discussion "Measuring Agility" in Chapter 10, Measuring Transformation Progress and Value.

CHAPTER 6

Nature of Future War

Future war can be envisioned as consisting of three general classes of activities. First, there is the perfection of traditional combat. Second, there is the evolution of what has been called nontraditional missions, a very mixed bag of activities including humanitarian assistance, SOLIC (Special Operations and Low Intensity Conflict) operations, counter-drug operations, peace operations, and counter-proliferation. Third, there is the birth of a form of war unique to the Information Age.

Information technology will not only change the nature of what we know today as war and operations other than war (OOTW), but also will spawn a new set of activities that will become familiar to future generations as constituting warfare in the 21st century. Today we might have some difficulty in viewing this set of activities as war or as the concern or responsibility of militaries. Current planning and budgeting approaches, as well as research and development activities, find it difficult to address these aspects of the future since they are not extensions of existing military missions and responsibilities. However, in each of these three cases, information technologies and the adaptations to the capabilities they provide will shape the battlespace and redefine the possibilities.

Future Traditional Combat

The future conventional battlespace will be neither contiguous nor orderly. Tempo will be extraordinarily high by today's standards. Given expected improvements in weapons and command and control, if a target can be seen, it can be destroyed. It should be noted that, more than ever, simply being able to destroy a target does not mean that one should do so. A variety of other considerations will determine the appropriate action to take. Some of these considerations will be the possibility of collateral damage, the link between the target and the effects desired, and the availability of non-lethal means. Survival of targets will depend upon organic defensive capabilities, suppression, and stealth. Concepts of operation will center around massing effects[1] rather than forces.

Command and control involves dynamic tradeoffs between ensuring that Rules of Engagement (ROE) are followed, prioritizing targets, and minimizing the time required for shooters to pull the information they need.[2] While commanders will have the ability to exert more direct influence on shaping the battlespace, they may wish to not exercise this option. NCW theory argues that, in certain kinds of situations, it is more effective to opt for a network-centric or self-synchronizing approach with the commander focused on influencing the initial conditions of the engagement rather than micromanaging it. If the experience of other organizations holds, staffs (as we now know them) will be significantly reduced (and decentralized) as organizational structures flatten. Many commands will be automatically disseminated and incorporated in decision aids. Many decisions will be fully automated. Virtually all information will be distributed horizontally. In short, many significant changes will need to be made in the way we think about command and control to respond to the challenges of the Information Age. With this much change foreseen down the road, care must be exercised to ensure success, even for the set of missions that we know best.

Evolution of Nontraditional Missions

Since the end of the Cold War, the nation has looked to the DoD not only to reduce overall spending,[3] but also to undertake a more diverse set of roles, both at home and around the globe. The unique capabilities developed by the U.S. military to meet the global challenge posed by the Soviet Union and maintained to protect U.S. interests around the world are seen as national assets that can be employed beyond their traditional combat and combat service support roles. Global air- and sea-lift are important for disaster relief, crisis intervention, humanitarian assistance, and support to peace operations. Similarly, the secure global communications capacity of the U.S. military is a crucial asset in a wide range of situations. The capability of the military to surge from its training bases and to react rapidly when dangerous situations arise far exceeds the capacities of most civilian agencies for whom surge capacity is a slow and cumbersome process and crisis response is an alien practice.[4] These unique capabilities, combined with the absence of an urgent, traditional military threat have, until September 11, 2001, caused the nation to expect greater involvement by the DoD in nontraditional missions such as humanitarian assistance, maintaining law and order when local and state authorities cannot, disaster relief, as well as countering drug smuggling and the proliferation of weapons of mass destruction. The events of September 11, 2001, have shifted the priority from traditional combat to terrorism and dealing with nations that host and support terrorists. The DoD, as its first priority, must focus on the nexus of terror and WMD. Clearly, this is very different from a focus on traditional combat and will require changes that go well beyond those that are involved in any adaptations to Information Age technologies.

The international environment has also changed in ways that make nontraditional missions more likely and more diverse. Coalition operations are now the accepted norm rather than the exception. International organizations, particularly the United Nations, have become increasingly assertive and have pressed a vision of global interests in peace and cooperation. As the only remaining global superpower, the United States is expected to respond whenever international peace and harmony are threatened and the nations of the world feel action is needed. This has been interpreted to mean that the U.S. must lead when the peace is threatened, international crimes are committed, or human tragedy looms.

Parochial clashes and conflicts undercut this growing internationalism. Freed from the smothering constraints of communist governments, national movements in Eastern Europe and the former U.S.S.R. have proven willing to challenge the peace to seek independence. Clans and tribes in Africa have reasserted their interests, sometimes violently. Asia is the site of arms races and uncertain relations between nations. Domestic and international struggles for the long-term control of the Middle East oil wealth and the worldwide resurgence of fundamentalist Islam add to the dangerous international situation. Drug traffickers present a frustrating cross-border challenge. Recent attention has also focused on conflicts arising from environmental issues, particularly disputes over water rights, ocean areas, and transnational air pollution.

Perhaps most important, media coverage and recent successes have led to very high expectations about the performance of the U.S. military. Minimizing casualties, among both combat forces and civilians, is widely perceived as an important and achievable goal. At the same time, the military is expected to be effective by accomplishing missions precisely and quickly.

Warfare in the Information Domain

As the global society enters the Information Age, military operations are inevitably impacted and transformed. Satellite communications, video teleconferencing, battlefield facsimile machines, digital communications systems, personal computers, the Global Positioning System, and dozens of other transforming tools are already commonplace.

At the same time that the DoD has infused these technological advances into operations at an ever-increasing rate, the DoD has gone from being the driving force in information technology to being a specialty user. The DoD, by policy and by necessity, finds itself in a new situation, relying on commercial-off-the-shelf (COTS) technology in order to acquire and field cost-effective systems. The widespread proliferation of Information Age technology, as well as the DoD's increased reliance on COTS products, has contributed to a significant increase in our vulnerability.

The implications of warfare in the information arena (cyberspace) are enormous.[5] First, national homelands are no longer sanctuaries by virtue of convention, distance, geography, or terrain. Physical borders are meaningless in cyberspace. Homelands and citizens can be attacked directly and even anonymously by foreign powers, criminal organizations, or non-national actors such as ethnic groups, renegade corporations, or zealots. Traditional military weapons cannot be interposed between the information warfare threat and society. Even where traditional combat conditions exist (hostile military forces face one another in a terrain-defined battlespace), kinetic weapons are now only one part of the arsenal available to the adversaries. Indeed, electronic espionage and sabotage, psychological warfare attacks delivered via mass media,[6][7] digital deception, and hacker attacks on the adversaries' command and control systems have been used and will increasingly be used to neutralize traditional forces and contribute in their own right to a concentration of effects at the crucial time and place in the battlespace.

Warfare in the Information Age will require enormously complex planning and coordination, very near real-time, vastly improved situation awareness, and the ability to share this awareness. Decision support systems will be required to filter and fuse[8] information very rapidly to provide common operational pictures (COPs)[9] and perform simple plan extensions and revisions almost automatically. Massive database and information exchange capabilities will be needed to track both friendly and enemy situations as well as rehearse and forecast battlespace dynamics.

Accordingly, our dependence on information and the systems that produce it, carry it, and provide access to it will continue to grow. This reality of an ever-increasing dependence on information means that the U.S. military must be able to:

1. Protect its own information systems;

2. Attack and influence the information systems of its adversaries; and

3. Leverage U.S. information advantages to gain a competitive advantage in the domain of national security.

---

[1]The word *fires* was used in the original text. The word *effects* has been substituted here to reflect current thinking re: effects-based operations. It can no longer be assumed that the destruction of targets is an end unto itself.

[2]The original manuscript called for "minimizing the time required to pass information from sensor to shooter." I have changed this because of the inherent shortcomings of a push-orientation. In a network-centric environment, a pull philosophy works better.

[3]Since the events of 9/11, the budget climate has changed considerably. But then, so too have the challenges. It could be argued that even with significantly more funds, the DoD will be hard pressed to prepare for and meet all of the challenges ahead.

[4]Hayes, Margaret Daly and Gary F. Wheatley, eds. *Interagency and Political-Military Dimensions of Peace Operations: Haiti—A*

Case Study. Washington, DC: National Defense University. February 1996.

[5]Alberts, David S. *Defensive Information Warfare.* Washington, DC: National Defense University. August 1996.

[6]Combelles Siegel, Pascale. *Target Bosnia: Integrating Information Activities in Peace Operations.* Washington, DC: CCRP and National Defense University. January 1998.

[7]Wentz, Larry, ed. *Lessons from Bosnia: The IFOR Experience.* Washington, DC: CCRP and National Defense University. April 1998. pp. 167-187.

[8]In many instances, and perhaps the rule rather than the exception, the push philosophy implied by "filter and fuse" will not work as effectively as a "post and pull" mechanism. For the moment the reader should consider the filter and fuse function to be performed at the behest of the user of the information—a subcontractor value-added service—rather than a hierarchical construct.

[9]COPs are not really a common picture, rather they are all about the consistency of the underlying data information, and the ability to have "views" that can be tailored by participants to support their different roles and responsibilities.

CHAPTER 7

Information Age Militaries

M ilitary operations in the future will be conducted by Information Age organizations. Unlike today's military organizations that would be reasonably familiar and comfortable to 19th-century warriors, Information Age militaries will be more of a reflection of contemporary private sector organizations. Information Age militaries will differ from 20th-century militaries with respect to their (1) strategy, (2) degree of integration, and (3) approach to command and control.

Strategy

Military strategy has, until recently, been basically symmetric with the aim of degrading and/or defeating an adversary's military forces. To some extent, military operations have been a separate phase in a conflict that begins when the political leadership turns to a military organization and expects it to undertake and accomplish a given military mission. Upon the conclusion of this mission (e.g., surrender of the enemy), the military retires and the political leadership takes over. This is not to say that civilian leadership is not engaged during the entire military phase, but that the role of civilian leadership during the conduct of military operations is more of an oversight role, not an operational one.

Conflicts in the Information Age will not have distinct military phases to the same extent as before. Military objectives will need, more than ever before, to be dynamically balanced with a set of nonmilitary objectives and subject to a complex set of constraints. Hence, military strategy will need to adjust to being a part of a larger operation and switch to an effects-based strategy (as opposed to an attrition-based strategy). The term *effects-based operations* (EBO) is relatively recent, although one would hope that warfare has always been about creating effects. However, in the Industrial Age, attrition effects became an automatic substitute for the ultimate objectives of military operations. As nontraditional military missions became more commonplace, it became obvious that new measures of effectiveness for military operations needed to be developed. Enemy attrition and loss-exchange ratios were no longer useful. EBO is simply a recognition of this. Its proponents are arguing for an explicit enunciation of the objectives of a military operation, how these military objectives relate to overall U.S. or coalition objectives, and the cause-effect relationships that link military actions to effects to military objectives to mission objectives. Normalcy indicators, for example, may be used to ascertain when a peacekeeping mission achieves the desired effects. In these cases, military actions (e.g., patrols, weapons confiscation) need to be related to normalcy. Killing people and breaking things may, in fact, be part and parcel of an effects-based strategy, but this connection should not be casually assumed. Much has been written on this change in the relationship of the military to conflict.[1]

Command and Control: Integrated Operations

While the Information Age will complicate military strategy, it will revolutionize military organizations and the approach to command and control. Command and control is a military term for leadership and management.[2] Improvements in Information Age technologies have changed the economics of information and hence, have altered its practical richness, reach, and the quality of the interactions among individuals and groups. As a result,[3][4] the nature of the fog and friction of war are being radically altered. This will enable us to move beyond the pursuit of blunder avoidance and deconfliction to achieving synergy on a routine basis in military operations.

Curiously, the term *integration* is not part of the dictionary definition of management, although it seems to me that a key component of management lies in its ability to integrate the actions of an organization. Information Age militaries will be able to generate synergy because they will be better integrated in a number of dimensions. These dimensions include echelon, coalition/joint, function, time, and geography.[5] The infinitive *to integrate* is commonly defined[6] as "to make a whole by bringing all parts together." Military operations traditionally break each of the dimensions mentioned above into parts that have for the most part not been brought together very well. This approach creates seams on the battlefield that an adversary can exploit. Military tactics recognize that the seam between units (particularly if the seam separates troops from different countries as they often did in World War II[7]) is a good place to attack. Information and opportunity find the cracks in the seams irresistible.

The real challenge in command and control is integration.[8] It is about getting a number of things to work toward a common purpose in a way that maximizes the totality of the resources available. This raises an interesting point about integration. Is integration about the means employed, or is it only about the effects produced? Can an organization be integrated without achieving integrated effects? If an organization achieves integrated effects, is it integrated? Take the idea that is central to Information Age command and control, self-synchronization. Are self-synchronizing forces integrated? These questions are important because they help us focus attention in the right places. I would argue that self-synchronizing forces (e.g., those that achieve synchronized results by emergent behavior[9]) are indeed integrated[10] because, in the final analysis, they achieve integrated effects by enabling individuals to develop synergistic behaviors. Synchronized behavior can also be a product of centralized planning and execution, or of centralized planning and decentralized execution. The way command and control should be exercised in the Information Age depends upon what actually works best in the set of circumstances and challenges we associate with today's and tomorrow's military missions.[11]

Information Age missions will be characterized by a large degree of unfamiliarity and complexity, and by exacting time pressures and constraints. They will require rapid,[12] decisive, and precise responses. The ability to rapidly respond is limited by physics unless one shifts to an approach involving the massing of the desired effects rather than the massing of forces. This, in turn, means that forces can be geographically dispersed. Dispersion of forces may result from either the inability to mass physically in time or a desire to maintain separation to avoid being an attractive target. Being decisive involves, among other things, being able to select the right effects and develop a feasible approach for achieving them. This requires a high level of understanding of the situation. *Precise* means that each element or part of the force knows if, when, and how to act and has the capability to achieve the desired effects. Rapid, decisive, and precise responses can only be accomplished if we are able to bring all of the available information we have to bear and all available assets to bear in a timely manner. Thus, the conditions necessary for success in the Information Age revolve around an organization characterized by information flows that are not unduly constrained, where the key parts of the organization share awareness, and where acts of individual parts can be self-synchronized. These are characteristics that are associated with integrated processes. This can only be achieved by adopting a network-centric approach and command philosophy.

---

[1]Alberts, David S. and Daniel S. Papp, eds., *Information Age Anthology*. Washington, DC: National Defense University and CCRP. June 1997-March 2001. Vols 1-3.

[2]Alberts, David S. and Richard E. Hayes. *Command Arrangements for Peace Operations*. Washington, DC: National Defense University. May 1995. pp. 5-13.

[3]Alberts, David S., John J. Garstka, and Frederick P. Stein. *Network Centric Warfare: Developing and Leveraging Information Superiority*. Washington, DC: CCRP. August 1999.

[4]Alberts, David S., John J. Garstka, Richard E. Hayes, and David A. Signori. *Understanding Information Age Warfare*. Washington, DC: CCRP. August 2001.

[5]*Ibid*. pp.148-157.

[6]*Webster's II New Riverside University Dictionary*. New York: Riverdale Publishing Company. 1984.

[7]October 23 to November 3, 1942—Superior British armor and air forces assaulted a combined Italian-German line in Egypt commanded by Marshal Rommel. The British succeeded in devastating several inferior Italian units, thus allowing the British armor to penetrate the line of defense, destroy the entire Italian division, and force the German Panzer division to retreat.

[8]Motivation, as well as process, is part of it.

[9]The concept of emergent behavior comes from the field of complex adaptive systems.

[10]A similar argument can be made for the meaning of *joint*.

[11]Although a robustly networked force is expected to significantly enhance shared situational awareness and thus enable self-synchronization to occur, it would be a mistake to conclude that self-synchronization is therefore the answer to all command and control challenges. Instead, moving to NCW enables self-synchronization and hence, provides the commander and the organization with an option that is certain to prove effective in many situations.

[12]Rapidity is not an end in itself. The objective is to be able to react as quickly as possible to provide a commander with a choice regarding the pace of battle and the time and place for decisive engagement.

CHAPTER 8

Adverse Consequences

NCW, as a manifestation of an Information Age transformation of the DoD, will bring about a series of changes that will profoundly affect both the nature of the information available to participants in a mission and how this information will be disseminated and used. The nature of an Information Age transformation of the military can be understood by comparing the nature of information flows, decisions, and command and control processes that have evolved from the Industrial Age to those which are characteristic of the Information Age. Industrial Age militaries have organizations, command structures, and sets of processes that have been adapted to the fog and friction of war.[1] These militaries are optimized for dealing with pervasive fog, a lack of information about the situation, and systemic friction, in part due to a lack of real-time communications and reliable equipment. Hence, Industrial Age military command decisions focus more on what is unknown or uncertain rather than what is known and understood. In Industrial Age militaries, decisions are most often driven by a desire to minimize regret rather than maximize expected value. Their concepts of operations are designed to be robust above all else. Their primary goal is to avoid blunders. In other words, in legacy military organizations, a strategy of risk avoidance prevails.

Figure 2 depicts the relationship between military effectiveness and the fog and friction of war. The shaded area depicts the region in which Industrial Age militaries operate.

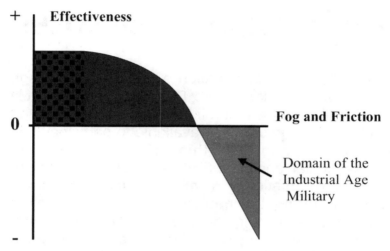

Figure 2. Fog, Friction, and Military Effectiveness

Information Age technologies have provided an opportunity to change this basic paradigm. Vastly improved battlespace information has, to a significant extent, lifted the fog of war.[2] And further improvements can be expected. Vastly improved communications, particularly a move from analog to digital and a move from point to point and broadcast to networking, allows us to share information in new ways, simultaneously increasing both its richness and reach.[3] The resultant increase that can be achieved in shared awareness will significantly reduce a major source of friction. Together, improvements in information quality and information dissemination have provided a firm foundation upon which network-centric operations can be built.

Figure 3 contrasts the nature of an Information Age DoD with that of an Industrial Age one. The prospect of the profound changes that would accompany a transformation from an Industrial Age military to an Information Age one has given rise to a number of concerns. Specifically, concerns have been voiced regarding the impacts of new and increased information flows on decisionmakers and changes to command processes. Other concerns focus on the new or increased vulnerabilities associated with reliance on Information Age systems and processes. Finally, a set of concerns centers on our ability to design and acquire secure, robust, reliable, coherent systems given the Information Age realities of increased reliance on COTS hardware and software and the ever-shrinking technology life cycle.

	Industrial Age	Information Age
Dealing with the Future	Predict/Plan Perfect Tasks	Prepare/Adapt Develop Agility
Developing Capabilities	Define Requirements Engineer Insert Technology Test Systems	Experiment Grow Coevolve MCPs Assess Operations
Command and Control	Do what I tell you Synchronize Control Constrain Subordinates Staff	Do what makes sense Self-synchronize Converge Enable Subordinates Collaborate
Dealing with Information	Push Use & Distribute Server-Client Clear People	Pull Post Before Process Peer to Peer Sanction Transaction

Figure 3. Characteristics of an Information Age DoD

The remainder of this chapter is devoted to a discussion of these concerns and their remedies, organized in the following manner:

- Information overload;

- Dynamics of information dissemination;

- Impact on military decisionmaking;

- Vulnerabilities arising from the information systems themselves; and

- Command and control design and acquisition issues.

Information Overload

A major concern that is frequently expressed and clearly needs to be addressed is that of nonessential information swamping critical information. The argument goes that the sheer volume of information received could frustrate a person's or organization's ability to quickly identify critical information for the decision at hand. This concern is founded upon an assumption that the push philosophy of information management will continue to prevail. A shift to a pull approach, where users get to shape their information space, clearly reduces the probability that users will get swamped with information of little or no relevance. Users must, in order to avoid situations in which more information than can be processed is presented, make decisions about what information is really needed, what is nice to have, what is irrelevant, and what is potentially distracting or confusing. Furthermore, they must determine when to stop collecting and waiting for information and when to take action. This decision is a function of residual uncertainty and the risks associated with the available options as a function of time. The user is clearly in a better position to make these decisions than some other party or parties. But moving to a pull approach is not a panacea. The question, however, shifts from "how does one sort through a pile of information to find out what is useful?" to "how does one know what information is available so that it can be pulled?"

The requirement for information clearly depends upon both the mission and the situation. Unless individuals are given an opportunity to think through what they really need, when they need it, and have an opportunity to practice (perhaps at "decision ranges"), expressed requirements for information will always be incomplete on the one hand and inflated on the other hand. There will be a tendency toward overkill in areas that we grasp and a lack of stated requirements for the unknown unknowns. Individuals with appropriate military experience must be placed in realistic situations and must be allowed to experiment with different amounts and types of information. The lessons learned from these experiments can be used as inputs to doctrine development, requirements, system design analyses, and the design of training. These experiments and training activities can be used, initially, to educate users regarding what information is available, how to locate it, and how to use it. Shifting from a push to a pull orientation shifts the focus from an ultimately losing strategy to a winning strategy. This is because it is simply impossible for a producer of information to know all of the people who may need this information and what they are going to do with it. It is not, however, impossible to have users learn what types of information are available from which sources and, eventually, to make good judgments about the reliability of various sources under various circumstances.

Better education and training devoted to information processing under stress and in environments characterized by uncertainty are needed to develop the necessary skills to handle these information-rich situations. Practice is key to perfecting and maintaining the skills necessary to function in a fast-paced, information-intensive environment. Therefore, exercises, on-the-job training, and continuing professional education need to be added to complete the necessary set of remedies for increases in the amounts of information that will be provided.

Sophisticated presentations can also obscure vital information and/or mask poor quality or incomplete data. Designing presentations that illuminate issues and facilitate decisionmaking involves tradeoffs and choices between raw (or unprocessed) data and information that contains a mixture of fact and inference. Often, fusion algorithms or decision aids fill in the blanks and provide users with inferences from available data. In some cases, valuable information is lost in the process. Thus, processing information can destroy information as it creates information. Given that producers of information cannot possibly know all of the uses of the information they collect, nor the importance of various details or lack of details, the current approach of guessing what users need should be re-examined. The remedies to address this concern include shifting to a paradigm of posting before processing,[4] in addition to the development of better visualization techniques to enable individuals to understand better the nature of the underlying data for a given presentation.

Uncertainty regarding the quality or integrity of the information being presented could lead to a lack of confidence that inhibits use of information or intelligence systems. Decisionmakers clearly need confidence in the reliability, currency, and accuracy of data in order to act on it. In the Information Age, the integrity and authenticity of data are increasingly of concern and the attributes of information[5] should be considered as part of any requirements analyses, acquisition processes, and training regiments.

In addition to the remedies discussed above, effective defensive protection measures and decision aids need to be developed that can permit decisionmakers to develop confidence and to rely on the authenticity and integrity of the data. Presentation techniques that convey the quality of the underlying data are an important issue in their own right.

Dynamics of Dissemination

Not only is the amount of information available dramatically increasing as the Information Age unfolds, but our ability to widely disseminate this information is keeping pace. As information sources proliferate, individuals are increasingly receiving inputs from multiple sources in a less-than-coordinated manner. This raises a number of issues. The first is associated with the separation of information flows from the chain of command. The second addresses disorderly and unpredictable flows.

Freeing information flows from the command chain means that commanders cannot control what subordinates see or know. Without appropriate changes to the way that military missions are conducted, this could create more fog and friction as a result of the disconnects among participants at different echelons. Behaviors might become less predictable, operations less synchronized, and risks made more difficult to manage. The command and control concepts and processes inherent in NCW serve to remedy this concern. This is because NCW is based upon a new model of command and control, one that features sharing of information (synchronization in the information domain[6]) and the collaborative processes to achieve a high degree of shared situational awareness. Thus, despite the variety of sources of information, the sharing of information and the collaboration enabled by the networked force combine to reduce the number and severity of the disconnects that might otherwise occur. An additional benefit is the increase in the richness of the awareness created. This increase in richness occurs as a result of the efforts to reconcile differences in fact and/or perspective that result from (1) more sources of information, (2) increased sharing of information, and (3) collaboration.

But other problems still remain. Asynchronous arrival of information has been found to confuse and distract decisionmakers. Studies have also shown that the weight individuals place upon information may be related to the order in which that information is received. This is potentially dangerous because it can lead to differences in individuals' perceptions of a situation, even if all of the participants have exactly the same information.

NCW virtually ensures that individuals will be receiving different information in different sequences. To avoid the potential pitfalls associated with this phenomenon, education, training, and practice are needed to heighten awareness of these issues and help individuals assimilate new data into their information domains. A sufficiently common perception of command intent is needed to ensure that behavior is consistent across the organization. Collaborative environments and tools will contribute to a group's ability to reconcile different perceptions. In addition, display techniques can facilitate information collection and analysis, and decision aids can help synthesize and fuse information on a continuing basis.

As with many of the concerns raised, practice is a key element of a remedy. In this case, practice is needed to ensure that individuals develop and maintain proficiencies in dealing with the potentially confusing phenomenon of asynchronous information flows.

Given the capabilities that will be coming online in the coming years, there will be an enormous increase in the amount of information coursing through communication pipes. A mix of information push and pull, with an increasing emphasis on pull, will improve our ability to anticipate and control requests for information. If this less orderly behavior is not accommodated, it could result in system degradation, particularly in times of great stress. In these situations, vital as well as nonvital information flow may be affected. To avoid this potentially crippling scenario, appropriate policy, doctrine, and procedures[7] regarding the use of information retrieval mechanisms need to be developed and instituted. Again, education, training, and practice are required to raise awareness of the problem and to develop the skills needed to operate in a degraded information environment. Network tools are also needed to provide warnings when the limits of the distribution system are being approached and to help bring the situation under control. Finally, the design of our information distribution infrastructure needs to maximize robustness and flexibility. The only certainty is that systems will not be used exactly as intended or under precisely the conditions assumed in their design, development, and testing.

Decisionmaking

The linkages between information quality, distribution, communications patterns, and decisionmaking are complex and diverse. This was true when our approach focused upon a small number of decisionmakers and a large number of executors. A review of organization theory, group dynamics, information theory, and past research on command and control offers key insights into these linkages and how they might function if current command concepts, organization, doctrine, and processes are not altered.

First, when information is freely available, role overlap tends to be commonplace. Superiors have a tendency (or are at least tempted) to micromanage, particularly when the stakes are high; and there are no higher stakes than combat. Subordinates, however, when provided with the larger picture historically available only to senior commanders, are also likely to second-guess decisions made at higher levels and (in richly connected systems) have the information required to undertake initiatives that their superiors may find surprising and perhaps inappropriate. Avoiding this set of counterproductive behaviors and management practices requires rethinking processes and organizational structures, as well as self-discipline and training.

Second, decisionmaking in an information rich environment increasingly means media attention. The pressures of a fish bowl environment affect performance in a variety of adverse ways. Tendencies to overreact, to act quickly, to appear decisive despite limited information, or to posture for the media can only be overcome through realistic training and experience.

When decisionmaking becomes a collective process, which tends to occur when several principals have easy access to one another in a situation that they all consider important, decisions tend to converge on options that meet group consensus. This collective wisdom has been demonstrated in both theoretical and empirical analyses to tend strongly toward risk adverse options or poorly developed group-think alternatives. The brilliant alternative or innovative approach foreseen by one individual is unlikely to survive this deliberative process. The potential strength of this collective process, which has excelled at solving complex problems such as those at operational and strategic combat levels, can only be achieved by an open approach to decisionmaking and a command approach that stresses individual innovation and leadership at all levels.

Fully connected systems also reduce the need for detailed action coordination by commanders because they make available information that would have to be requested from other elements in a classic military information structure. For example, rather than having to request information about the availability of transportation assets or ammunition needed for a combat operation, a line commander will be able to check stock levels directly. This can lead to insufficient or ineffective coordination because subject matter experts are not consulted or because more than one commander makes plans to use the same asset, but none has a clear commitment of asset availability.

Industry experience with richly connected systems has shown that collaborative planning and decision aids (which automatically perform coordination tasks and/or pass information between nodes in decisionmaking structures) are needed to avoid these problems. In addition, red team procedures to cross-check decisions can help to ensure adequate, timely coordination.

As generations of military commanders who have become accustomed to the availability of high density and high quality data about the battlefield mature and move into senior command positions, the expectation of near perfect information and the willingness to delay decisions in the expectation of better information may grow. However, the very rapid pace of future battles, as well as the imperatives of turning inside adversary decision loops, will punish procrastination and inaction severely. The commander who waits for near perfect information will be defeated by one who acts on "good enough" information.

Future commanders must develop the judgement required to differentiate between sufficient and desirable information. Because of the increased pace of battle and the high lethality expected in future battlespace, more and more decisions will be assigned to expert systems. This will include not only sensor-to-shooter linkages where the identification, assignment, and engagement of targets must be so rapid that unaided human decisionmaking cannot keep pace, but also other complex domains characterized by rapid developments in logistics planning, air tasking order development, and medivac helicopter routing. However, development, testing, and training are, in and of themselves, currently inadequate to ensure confidence in these systems. Testing is particularly important. Technology demonstrations are a good, cost effective way to gain user feedback and to develop positive attitudes toward these systems, but operational testing in realistic field conditions is also necessary to avoid system failures or lack of use in the field. Failure during early field experience will poison attitudes that can only be overcome slowly and at great expense. Thus, care must be taken to involve users early on in the design process.

Finally, by their very nature as automatons, computer systems have no inherent ability to recognize their own limitations. When applied in inappropriate circumstances, they will produce answers that may be logical, but incorrect. The entire process, from concept through design, testing, and doctrine development, must include a recognition of this inherent problem. Ultimately, humans must make sound decisions about when and under what circumstances to rely on automated systems.

This discussion has been focused on the logical evolution of traditional combat. The military is familiar and comfortable with traditional combat and it is not hard to envision how military organizations and decisionmaking behavior need to adapt in the future. However, the situations we are most likely to face are far less familiar. This exacerbates the problems that have been raised and significantly increases the challenges associated with managing information and decisionmaking.

Vulnerabilities

As the sophistication of the military information systems support structure grows over time, the inherent vulnerabilities will become more important. Planning and practice can minimize these vulnerabilities, but they cannot be safely ignored. First, all military equipment is in danger of capture. Even rear areas are raided to capture or destroy vital elements of important systems. Hence, steps must be taken to prevent equipment loss, to ensure that losses are known, and to frustrate enemy exploitation of captured systems. Unique keys that identify and authorize users on particular systems, devices that report current locations on key hardware items via satellite, authentication procedures, and security codes will be important defensive systems. Doctrine and training necessary to ensure their proper use will also be necessary.

As the Global Information Grid and its capabilities proliferate in the battlespace, vulnerabilities will increase because: (a) the number of valid users with access to the system rises, magnifying the insider threat; (b) the number of nodes and connection points grows, providing adversaries with more opportunities to penetrate the system from the outside; and (c) if a compromise does occur, the perpetrator will have access to more information than would have been available in the past.

Indeed, as the force becomes increasingly networked, the mere task of noticing a penetration or penetration attempt becomes ever more difficult. Often system problems cannot be readily diagnosed as either natural or the product of information warfare attacks. Even a single penetration can be extremely damaging, particularly in a richly connected information system.

Obviously, some data (such as concepts of operations, planning documents, and orders) are extremely sensitive. A well-crafted worm or computer virus can spread literally at the speed of light once inside a complex system. Moreover, the knowledge that databases have been penetrated and may be corrupted can greatly inhibit decisive and effective decisionmaking. New types of defensive decision aids will be needed to detect, assess, and counter such attacks.

Although not a new phenomenon, misinformation, even a small amount of it, can negate the benefits of increased quantity and quality of information. Before, it could be reasonably (although not without some risk) assumed that the information received through the chain of command was not misleading (or at least purposefully so). With the freeing of the information flows from the chain of command and the introduction of many new and perhaps unproven sources of information, this benign information environment can no longer be assumed. Again, NCW principles contribute to an ability to spot, question, and hopefully deal with misinformation. Bringing more brains to bear increases the likelihood that the wheat gets separated from the chaff and that the razor blades (sources of danger) are harmlessly removed.

Command and Control Design and Acquisition

Because the inventory of information systems will inevitably continue to undergo rapid development and replacement, the design and acquisition of these systems become crucial in the defense against many vulnerabilities.

As they focus on definitive, exhaustive testing against technical and often arcane specifications, traditional test and evaluation procedures have developed a bad reputation in the operational community for often preventing the adoption of an imperfect but acceptable system. Technology demonstrations have emerged as a way of exposing new systems to operators and operational conditions without having to address arcane testing standards. Reliance on demonstrations alone can be equally unhealthy because it encourages adoption of systems that have not really been tested at all. More robust, integrated, and operationally-oriented processes of user assessment, as well as realistic applications (including baselines and benchmarks to ensure new systems add measurable capability), are needed.

The DoD's increasing reliance on COTS hardware and software increases vulnerabilities by making military systems familiar to sophisticated adversaries and by exposing them to software developers and technicians who are not subject to security regulations. Hence, design and acquisition procedures need to consider security and minimize exposure. Indeed, some systems may be too sensitive to rely on COTS designs or procurements.

The DoD's increasing reliance on COTS products is also having a deleterious impact on the U.S. Government's in-house capability to maintain the expertise required to adapt COTS systems and create capabilities not needed by the commercial sector. The engineering base required to meet military standards is an essential element of COTS product reliance strategy. A coherent program designed to maintain and exercise this capacity is needed. At least part of this program could be devoted to the post-deployment support of information systems. In many cases, these systems will need to be revised in order to maintain interoperability with new systems, a process that necessitates the linkage of COTS systems with military requirements. This means not only building linkages between systems, but also having the capacity to reengineer the systems and the processes that the systems support.

Because command and control systems are never complete and will be continuously undergoing transitions, the ability to maintain mission capability while upgrading or integrating systems also remains crucial. This capability requires planning and creativity. The Army's concept of selecting one unit as a living test bed for new ideas and equipment and fielding only what is successful in the chosen environment represents one approach to this problem. Other approaches, such as parallel operation of new and old systems during a test period, may be attractive in some circumstances.

Finally, COTS product reliance in military systems is very different from relying on commercial systems. Plans for the DoD to rely on commercial satellite communications systems must recognize that other clients can make demands on these systems and may limit the DoD's access to them in times of crisis. Moreover, commercial services are not always designed for graceful degradation or fully backed up in the event of system failure. Hence, basic availability will be an issue when relying on commercial systems, particularly in times of crisis, and needs to be addressed (a) when contractual arrangements are made and (b) when contingency planning is done for crises.

---

[1]Clausewitz, Carl von. Trans. By Peter Paret. *On War.* New York: Knopf. 1993.

[2]This is not to say that we will have anything approaching "total situational awareness," but to say that we can move from a mindset preoccupied with what we do not know to one where we can focus on leveraging what we do know.

[3]Magretta, Joan. "The Power of Virtual Integration: An Interview with Dell Computer's Michael Dell." *Harvard Business Review*. 76:2 (March-April 1998), pp. 72-84.

[4]The use of the term *processing* has generated a considerable amount of discussion centered on the issue of what basic processing is necessary to make the information useful. The intent of this policy is to make the information available in as timely a way as possible and not to destroy information that someone else would find useful by too much processing/aggregation.

[5]The attributes of information are discussed in: Alberts, David S., John J. Garstka, Richard E. Hayes, and David A. Signori. *Understanding Information Age Warfare*. Washington, DC: CCRP. August 2001. pp. 108-115.

[6]A discussion of the information domain and the other domains of war can be found in: Alberts, David S., John J. Garstka, Richard E. Hayes, and David A. Signori. *Understanding Information Age Warfare*. Washington, DC: CCRP. August 2001. pp. 10-15.

[7]While one can expect that network management (centralized and distributed) tools and techniques will improve, it would not be prudent to rely solely on technology alone to solve this problem.

CHAPTER 9

Strategy for Transformation

The concerns identified and discussed in the last chapter are serious ones. Considering the enormous benefits that are associated with NCW, these potential pitfalls are not valid or sufficient reasons for deferring, delaying, or half-heartedly embracing Information Age concepts and technologies, particularly since the potential disruptions, dysfunction, and varied other problems associated with Information Age concepts and technologies can be avoided or successfully contained while significant benefits can be harvested.

Looking at the remedies identified to address each of these specific concerns, one finds a unifying theme—the danger of failing to recognize that existing mindsets, practices, and processes must give way to new mindsets, practices, and processes that are in tune with the new characteristics of information and its dissemination. That is, a recognition that exposure to new information technologies and their capabilities is potentially dangerous[1] unless it is accompanied by changes in a number of key dimensions. Further, a recognition that the changes that are required are interrelated and hence, need to be considered in a holistic manner. They need to be coevolved.

A review of the discussion of concerns indicates that changes need to occur in all of the following:

- Concepts of operation;

- Command and control approach and processes;

- Organization and doctrine;

- Battlespace entities;

- Systems; and

- Education, training, and exercises.

Mission Capability Packages

In order to accomplish a mission or task, a set of interrelated capabilities[2] are needed. This collection of the required capabilities can be thought of as a mission capability package.[3] The dimensions listed above constitute key elements of a mission capability package. A mission capability package thus consists of an operational concept and associated command approach, organization and doctrine, battlespace entities[4] and systems, education, training, and exercises. When one of these elements changes, it stands to reason that this will impact the organization's capability, for better or worse, to perform the mission at hand. The mission capability package approach moves the DoD away from a narrow focus on technology and systems[5]—what some have called the focus on "M" in DOTMLPF.[6]

Information technology helps us move beyond the current physical manifestations of systems and technology (platforms and headquarters) to a full consideration of all of the aspects of the military mission(s) to be supported. Mission capability packages encompass the full range of tools by which problems can be addressed or managed (from technical requirements to training) and as such hold the key to success in efforts to transform the force. The mission capability package approach moves us from an emphasis on what we buy to what we do. In the Information Age, what we buy and what we do are inexorably intertwined as never before.

The transformation of the DoD will involve mission capability packages that are characterized by their inherent jointness and by their network-centricity. The transformation of the DoD will also involve a transformation of the processes that give rise to these mission capability packages including budgeting and planning processes, acquisition and testing processes (particularly those involved in providing the infostructure[7 8]), logistics, and personnel management. The next chapter discusses the new process needed to conceive, mature, test, and implement mission capability packages.

Coevolving Mission Capability Packages

The mission capability package approach (depicted in Figure 4) begins with a clearly defined mission or set of missions and seeks to understand, without preconceived notions or solutions, (a) what is required to complete the mission(s) successfully and (b) how those requirements may differ from current force structure, command and control arrangements, organizations, doctrine, and technologies. Potential solutions, or initial mission capability package concepts, are developed in the concept development phase based on prior research, lessons learned, expert judgment, and most importantly, discovery experiments. Their strength lies in their thoroughness and coherence.

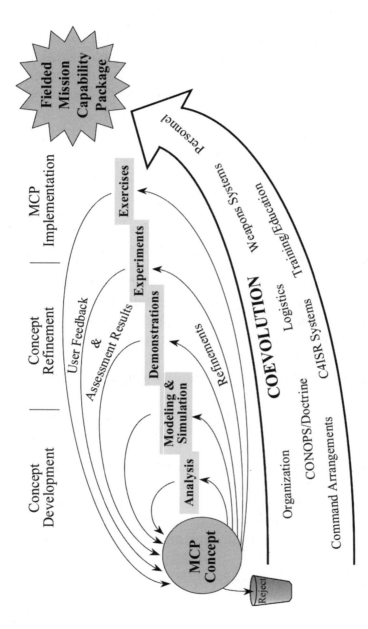

Figure 4. Mission Capability Package Coevolution

The mission capability package approach calls for exposing an initial mission capability package concept to review and critique by the operational community and domain experts early and often in order to refine and improve the concept. This review may take the form of demonstrations, experiments, exercises, simulations, modeling, or expert criticism. All of these will be needed for major initiatives. What matters is that as the concept matures, the process becomes increasingly focused and the mission capability package concept is refined based upon empirical evidence. As consensus and supporting evidence emerge, the refinement process is transformed into an evolutionary process characterized by a build-a-little, test-a-little philosophy that embodies the principles of evolutionary acquisition.[9]

Finally, the mission capability package moves into its implementation phase. This implementation phase is also comprehensive in nature. Systems may be built, but not in isolation. Doctrine development, command reorganization, relevant professional military education and training, as well as the technical systems themselves are all specified. This process has the comprehensiveness, coherence, and orientation necessary to transform ideas and technologies into real operational capabilities while avoiding adverse unintended consequences. Hence, mission capability packages are the recommended vehicle to ensure effective remedies and minimize risk.

---

[1]Prior to 1995, the prevailing opinion was that it was desirable that the introduction of new IT capabilities be accompanied by changes in processes because these changes would enhance the return on investment. The 1995 analysis recognized that the

problem was more than giving up potential ROI and that, in fact, changes were needed to prevent dysfunctional behaviors that could adversely affect performance.

[2]One might find it strange to refer to a concept or an organization as a capability. In fact, a concept represents the glue that holds the other capabilities together and an organization possesses a number of characteristics that enable it to accomplish various tasks that individually and collectivity represent capabilities.

[3]*Joint Vision 2020* and other DoD publications utilize the term DOTMLPF to refer to a mission capability package. To some, this term serves to reenforce the stovepiped nature of these communities, and does not adequately emphasize the need for a new concept of operations, new command approach, and new processes.

[4]Alberts, David S., John J. Garstka, and Frederick P. Stein. *Network Centric Warfare: Developing and Leveraging Information Superiority*. Washington, DC: CCRP. August 1999. p. 125.

[5]It has become increasingly recognized that our planning, investment, and acquisition processes focus almost exclusively on the big "M" in DOTMLPF. There are various proposals for addressing this imbalance—Joint Chiefs of Staff. *CJCS Strategic Plan*. February 20, 2002. (For Official Use Only).

[6]Doctrine, Organization, Training, Materiel, Leadership, Personnel, and Facilities.

[7]*Information Superiority—Making the Joint Vision Happen*. Washington, DC: Department of Defense. 2000.

[8]*Network Centric Warfare Department of Defense Report to Congress*. July 2001. pp. 5-12.

[9]AFCEA Study Team. *Command and Control Systems Acquisition Study Final Report*. Falls Church, VA: AFCEA. November 8, 1982.

CHAPTER 10

Measuring Transformation Progress and Value

This section begins by looking at the basic characteristics of an Information Age organization, characteristics that could be used to measure progress toward a transformed organization. It continues with a discussion of the nature of the journey to a transformed organization, identifies specific milestones along the way, and suggests metrics that can be used to measure progress and value.

Characteristics of an Information Age Organization

An Information Age military will differ in many respects from its Industrial Age counterpart. These changes are primarily concentrated in four dimensions—mission space (what the military is called upon to do), environment (the conditions, constraints, and values that govern military operations), concept (the military business model), and the way the organization provides and supports value creation (the business side of the DoD). This book is focused primarily on the third of these dimensions, leaving discussions of mission space and environment to political-military experts. The focus on this third dimension is justified because it is how we create value in the competitive space of national security and because of the uncertainty that surrounds future threats and geopolitical environments. This change in emphasis is being reflected in a change in the basis for U.S. strategy defense planning—a move from a threat-based to a capabilities-based model.

The ability of an organization to develop and utilize information is clearly one of the most important determinants of success. Quality information, the widespread sharing of this information, and command approaches that enable self-synchronization contribute to agility. In times when there is so much uncertainty about the mission space and the environment, agility is a highly desirable attribute. One could argue that increased agility is an attribute of the force that should be sought even if it means sacrificing some specific functionality. Given what is increasingly referred to as an "uncertain future," does it make sense to become extremely well-versed in one particular set of tasks, only to find that we are actually needed to perform a different set of tasks?

It is worth repeating the initial line from the 2000 *NCW Report to Congress*, "Network Centric Warfare is no less than the embodiment of an Information Age transformation of DoD."[1] There is a direct connection between an organization's agility and its ability to bring all of its information to bear in developing an understanding of a situation and all of its assets to bear in responding to a situation. For this reason, a business model based on these characteristics is ideal for an Information Age military. Network Centric

Warfare is a military business model (a way to create a competitive advantage and value) that has these desirable characteristics. Thus, the transformation to an Information Age business model is inseparable from progress toward network-centric operations.

Network-centric concepts need not only to be applied to warfighting (or more generally to the various missions and tasks the DoD will be called upon to do), but they also need to be applied to the business side of the DoD. The DoD must be viewed and analyzed holistically. A mission capability package approach to each mission or task is the only way to ensure that capabilities can properly coevolve and that all of our information and assets can be rapidly brought to bear as we undertake the wide range of tasks that lie ahead. Hence, the value calculus for the DoD needs to include a synthesis of what was formerly known as "tooth and tail" and have mission capability packages as their basic unit.

Previous distinctions between "tooth and tail" no longer serve their original purpose and have become a distraction in a network-centric world. Infrastructure as something that intrinsically needs to be minimized is also an outdated concept. The notions of "tooth to tail" ratios and the association of infrastructure with overhead need to be replaced with the concept of a value chain. In a network-centric world, a robustly networked force is not infrastructure (or tail) to be reduced, but an enabler of the Information Age business model. A robustly networked force is an enabler whose value cannot be considered in isolation from the other links in the value chain. Its absolute size (cost) is not relevant. Rather, it is the return on investment (ROI) and how this return compares to other potential investments that matter. In the Information Age, investments in information, its collection, distribution, and related investments in analysis, presentation, and protection can only be judged in a mission capability context.

Measuring Agility

Agility was defined as a key characteristic of an Information Age organization; a characteristic to be sought even at the sacrifice of seeking to perfect capabilities associated with specific missions or tasks. Agility is, of course, of paramount importance in an uncertain world. Given that the focus of this book has been on the ability to conduct military operations, it stands to reason that agile command and control would be a fundamental force capability and a scenario-independent measure that is directly related to NCW capability.

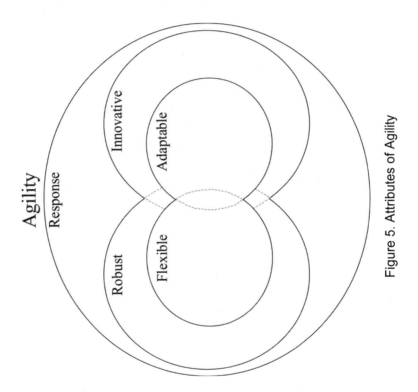

Figure 5. Attributes of Agility

Agility (see Figure 5) is a property of an individual or organization that has a synergistic combination of the following attributes: robustness, flexibility, innovativeness, adaptiveness, and responsiveness. These relate to the variety of circumstances under which an organization can be effective. Robustness is the ability to maintain effectiveness across a range of missions or tasks, circumstances, and conditions. It includes the ability to maintain effectiveness under attack and when damaged and/or degraded, as well as across the spectrum of conflict. Flexibility is the ability to envision multiple ways of accomplishing a task and/or conceiving of different paths to an objective. This means the ability to switch between alternatives as appropriate. Adaptiveness is inwardly focused. It is the ability to change the way one does business in an effort to improve performance in the face of changes in the environment. Innovativeness is the ability to learn about missions and operating environments and create novel approaches to create and maintain competitive advantages. Responsiveness is the ability to react appropriately in a timely manner. These definitions are only preliminary. Efforts are currently underway to settle on definitions for these terms and develop measures and/or indicants that could be used.[2]

Agile command and control focuses upon an organization's ability to provide dynamic command intent and direction at an appropriate level of detail to synchronize effects. This begins with the ability to assemble and deploy a needed command and control capability and make modifications to this capability as required. Command and control capabilities include the dimensions of richness, reach, and richness of interaction. Richness relates to information sources and the attributes of information related to the information provided by these sources.[3] Reach includes network topology, performance characteristics, robustness of the network, and security. The richness of the interactions refers to the nature of the communications (information transfers) supported, and the measures of the ability to assemble, deploy, and adjust command and control capabilities including speed of initial deployment, speed and quality of adjustment, and the ability to maintain robustness. The second dimension addresses the level of interoperability (integration) that can be achieved. The third dimension deals with the characteristics of the command approach. The same measures that would apply to the force as a whole are put into a command and control context. For example, instead of addressing the ability of the force to be responsive in unfamiliar situations, agile command and control involves the ability to provide intent and direction in unfamiliar situations.

The use of agility as a prime measure of force effectiveness moves the discussion from a threat-based focus to a capabilities-based focus. Instead of being assessed on how well a unit does on a scripted exercise, units will be assessed on their overall readiness to respond in an uncertain world.

The Journey to a Transformed Organization

The journey to a transformed organization requires development of (1) the ability to conduct NCW (by deploying network-centric mission capability packages) and (2) supporting processes that provide and support the development and deployment of network-centric mission capability packages.

The ability to conduct NCW is not an all or nothing proposition; it comes in varying degrees. A capability model for NCW that specifies five levels that represent increasing capability to conduct NCW was developed for *Understanding Information Age Warfare* and has been incorporated in the DoD's *NCW Report to Congress.*[4] This capability model is provided in Figure 6.

Command and Control

		Traditional	Collaborative Planning	Self-synchronization
	Shared Awareness		3	4
Developing Situation Awareness	Information Sharing	1	2	
	Organic Sources	0		

Figure 6. NCW Levels of Maturity

This capability model is based upon the two pillars of NCW: the development of shared awareness and the ability to capitalize on the shared awareness by moving to a command and control approach based upon self-synchronization. Five capability levels are depicted beginning with Level 0. Level 0 represents a traditional or hierarchical approach to command and control which, for the most part, is based upon information from organic sensors and systems. Organic here refers to a unit's or community's assets. Thus, in Level 0, information is not shared outside of pre-existing stovepipes and point-to-point flows. Moving to Level 1 involves a "post before use" strategy and a shift from push to pull that makes information far more widely available.[5] Moving to Level 2 involves moving from a passive sharing of information to a collaborative process focused on understanding the information (putting it into context) and the situation to develop a higher quality of awareness. Moving to Level 3 involves discussions (collaborations) that go beyond what the information is and means to what should be done about the situation. In other words, the beginnings of collaborative action. Finally, a move to Level 4 entails the adoption of a command approach rooted in the concept of self-synchronization.

Imbedded in this model is a logical migration path for developing network-centric mission capability packages. Once a move to Level 1 has been made, human nature, combined with the requirement to accomplish the mission, will drive organizational behavior to higher levels of capability when it is appropriate (as a function of the situation and the mission). Figure 7 depicts the migration path.

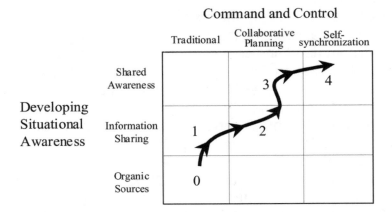

Figure 7. NCW Migration Path

Transformation Metrics

Given that the transformation of the DoD to an Information Age organization will take a considerable amount of time and effort,[6] it is imperative that we understand the nature and amount of progress that is being made and the types of investments that are paying dividends. This section discusses metrics that will be useful, both in measuring progress and in measuring the value to be associated with this progress.

Progress in transforming to an Information Age military is intimately associated with the nature of the network-centric mission capability packages being developed and fielded. Therefore, it stands to reason that the (1) NCW capability model, (2) NCW value chain,[7] and (3) inherent characteristics of Information Age organizations could serve as a basis for the development of transformation metrics.

The NCW capability model can be used to provide a snapshot, at any point in time, of where we are on the road to NCW capability. In addition, the capability model can also provide a leading indicator that presages the transformation of the force. For example, the attainment of a given level of capability in one mission area can signal the ability of the Department to achieve the same level of capability in other mission areas with similar characteristics and complexity.

Another way to measure progress is to employ the NCW value chain (Figure 8). The NCW value chain begins with a robustly networked force. The degree to which the force is clearly networked is related to the ability of the force to share information (extend its reach) and to its ability to collaborate. Both information sharing and collaborative capabilities contribute to the quality of the information (its richness), which in turn is related to the ability of the "mission organization"[8] to generate awareness. Information richness, reach, and the quality of interaction are related to the ability of the mission organization to achieve a high degree of shared awareness among the participants. Shared awareness is linked to the ability of the force to synchronize their effects, which is related to mission success. Hence, the NCW value chain incorporates a set of testable linkage hypotheses that can be explored and calibrated in experiments and analyses. In terms of the domains of warfare, a robustly networked force coupled with an ability to do both defensive and offensive information operations contributes to a force's capabilities in the information domain. When these are related to information needs (a property of the concepts of operations and command approach) and compared to the corresponding capabilities of our adversaries, the extent to which Information Superiority or an advantage in the information domain is achieved can be determined. A similar calculus in the cognitive domain (where awareness and decisionmaking are considered, rather than information) determines the party that has an advantage in the cognitive domain (decision superiority). The ability to turn advantages in the information and cognitive domains, the ability to leverage information and understanding to achieve an execution advantage, depends upon the concepts of operation, command approach, and weapons, or other means as appropriate.

Each of these links in the value chain can be measured and the degree to which they are related ascertained. Given that there are bound to be time lags between progress on one link and its reflection in later links, the NCW value chain, like the maturity model, can be used as both a snapshot measure and as a leading indicator of value.

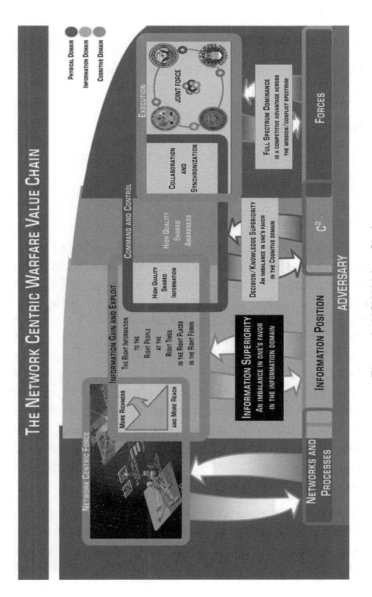

Figure 8. NCW Value Chain

It will be important to measure progress in a number of related areas. These include:

- Achievement of NCW capability;

- Putting the enablers of NCW in place;

- Understanding NCW;

- Realizing the value of NCW; and

- Transforming DoD processes to support transformation.

Achievement of NCW Capability

The Department is a very large and very complex organization with a wide variety of tasks and missions to accomplish. The metrics discussed above are rather easy to understand in the context of a particular task or mission. For example, it is somewhat straightforward to determine whether we can bring a network-centric capability to the task or mission at hand, and its maturity level. Thus, as time goes by, we can see if we are making progress as measured by increasing levels of maturity. But it is considerably more difficult to go from a task or mission context to the DoD as a whole. Clearly we will, at any given point in time, be able to perform some selected tasks at higher levels of maturity, but not others.

All tasks are not equal. The development of an aggregate measure for NCW maturity is feasible, but will involve either explicit or implicit assumptions about (1) the relative merits of achieving each level of maturity and (2) the relative importance of each of our tasks and missions. One approach is to take key missions and tasks (perhaps those specified in the Defense Planning Guidance as being transformation goals) and concentrate on moving these to a given level of maturity by some certain dates. One could also specify some minimum level (perhaps Level 1) and set a goal of achieving this for all DoD efforts by a certain date or simply measure what percent of a list of tasks and missions have achieved the various levels.

Putting the Enablers in Place

The most basic enabler of NCW is the "net" itself. The degree to which we have (or will have in place at some time in the future) an information network that enables NCW can be measured. Deploying a full set of network services throughout the DoD and extending this "net," or more accurately, a necessary subset of network services to others that the DoD needs to interact with, will take some time. In fact, it is probable that there will always be differences in the nature of the services afforded to networked entities. In order to understand the best strategy to use in deploying the "net," and in allocating resources among networked entities, we need to be able to characterize and value the connectivity and services available at any given point in time. Ultimately, we need a DoD-wide measure to reflect the potential value of the "net" to the DoD. This is because the value of the "net" to the DoD is more than the sum of the value of the "net" for a given set of missions.

However, we need to start with a mission-oriented measure.[9] Such a measure begins with the specification of the set of mission participants. Hence, the network will extend beyond our own forces to include non-U.S. military nodes, individuals, or organizations (e.g., other USG and coalition partners) that are key participants in a mission. A network consists of links and nodes. For a node to be "on the net" there must be an appropriate link available and the node must be "net ready."[10] For two or more nodes to interact, appropriate network services must also be available. These services include not only those needed to exchange information, for example, but also the services necessary to ensure that only legitimate exchanges take place in a protected environment. Hence, information assurance is fully integrated into the concept of network services. A simple but useful two-dimensional mission-oriented measure of the extent to which an "enabling network" is in place is provided in Figure 9.

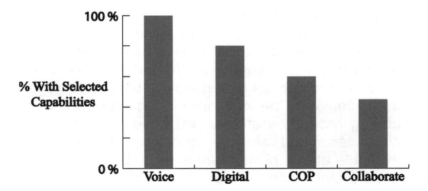

Figure 9. Measure of Network Capabilities

The first dimension corresponds to the reach of the network while the second dimension relates to the nature of the interchange supported (the richness of nodal interactions). In Figure 9, each bar represents the percentage of mission participants that are supported. In this case, everyone can have a voice conversation with each other, 80 percent of the mission participants can exchange digital information, 60 percent have access to the COP, but only 40 percent can participate in a collaborative environment. Developing a baseline for selected missions would not be very difficult and various experiments and analyses could be used to estimate the relationship between the provision of network services, the development of awareness and shared awareness, and other measures of mission performance and effectiveness. Thresholds could be empirically established (e.g., 60 percent of participants must be able to collaborate if a useful level of shared awareness is to be achieved) and used to map progress on the provision of network services to enable each of the levels of NCW maturity.

Please note that this is not a traditional measure of a network. Traditional measures focus on things like throughput and availability and do not take into consideration the nature of the behaviors that the network is supposed to support. This measure focuses on the information and NCW process-related capability that the network provides in the context of the participants of the mission.

In theory, the same measure could apply to the force as a whole. In practice, however, this would entail making some assumptions about the nature of the non-U.S. military participants that should be included in the calculation. Moreover, the mapping from this measure to overall force effectiveness could not be directly accomplished. The last link would need to be an extrapolation from a representative set of missions and circumstances.

Understanding Network Centric Warfare

Some have argued that we need not measure the progress we are making in understanding NCW because the only thing that matters is whether or not our ability to conduct missions is being improved. They argue that if we are getting value from our network and the adaptations of military operations that take advantage of Information Age concepts and technologies, then we clearly have a sufficient understanding of NCW.

However, we can derive real value from measuring progress. This is because the rate of progress that we can make depends, not on our ability to understand whether something works, but on why it works (or for that, matter why it does not work). If we try something and it works, we can implement it. To improve upon it, we would need to try something else and see if it works. This trial and error approach may eventually succeed, but it is not very efficient. Efficiency comes about as we increase our ability to understand the connections so we can try something we have good reason to believe will be an improvement. As our understanding grows, we are able to predict not only what will improve things, but by how much, and thus we are in a position to explore options theoretically before actually testing them empirically.

Therefore, we would greatly benefit by working on an NCW model while simultaneously developing and experimenting with NCW mission capability packages. The NCW model would embody our understanding of the relationships hypothesized by NCW theory. First, it will be necessary to establish that, in fact, these relationships exist in reality. Second, we need to understand the conditions under which the relationships hold. Third, we need to be able to calibrate (quantitatively) the relationships. Progress on an NCW model is synonymous with progress on our understanding.

How can one measure progress on a model of NCW? The following approach could be used to represent the degree of understanding we have achieved. The tenets of NCW could be used to define the major components of the model. Each tenet stipulates one or more cause-effect relationships (e.g., higher shared awareness leads to higher degree of synchronization). Associated with each of these relationships is an implied set of conditions (e.g., the command and control approach capitalized on shared awareness). These conditions are, in effect, a set of independent variables, some of which are controllable. Our understanding of a particular tenet is most directly reflected in the amount of variation that we can explain.[11] This value is determined empirically. The higher the value, the greater our understanding of the relationships (under the conditions that have been observed). The NCW tenets are themselves linked and their collective ability to predict the degree to which effects can be synchronized as a function of the key concepts of NCW can be used as a measure of the degree to which we understand NCW.

Please note that I have not tried to link the tenets of NCW to mission success or outcomes. That is because there are a great many variables that have nothing to do with a network-centric approach that can have a significant bearing on whether or not a mission is successful. Thus, adopting NCW principles does not guarantee success. Rather, it allows one to use the available information and the available assets more effectively.

If one wants to link NCW tenets to measures of mission success in order to determine value, then it needs to be a comparative analysis as discussed in the next section.

Realizing the Value of NCW

Making progress toward a Network Centric Warfare capability is important only if the achievement of this capability is accompanied by an increased ability to accomplish the myriad of tasks and missions that are assigned to the DoD. Assuming such a connection to value exists, measuring progress on the fundamental enabler of NCW, the "net," provides a leading indicator for the level of NCW maturity, which in turn provides a leading indicator of the value that will be realized by NCW.

Thus, the establishment of a definitive link between the achievement of network-centric capabilities and mission value is necessary if we are to rely upon the leading indicators to guide DoD policy and investments. This requires that we extend our NCW model by adding a set of metrics that allows us to validate and calibrate the last link in the NCW value chain. The NCW model provides us with metrics that reflect all but the last tenet of NCW (specifically, the quality of awareness, the degree to which it is shared, and the level of synchronization achieved). Whether or not these translate into mission success is dependent on many things. These include the means at our disposal to deal with the situation, the capabilities of our adversaries, environmental conditions, and among a long list of other factors, political constraints. To ascertain the actual value that can be attributed to these key NCW capabilities (e.g., the ability to share awareness), a series of comparative analyses or experiments that control for these numerous other factors needs to be performed. A set of metrics that reflect mission success need to be developed and a baseline case needs to be compared with one or more cases that differ with respect to one or more of the key NCW capabilities. Over the years, there have been a number of metrics that have emerged that serve as generally accepted measures for traditional combat missions (e.g., loss exchange ratios, time to accomplish a mission[12]). However, given the significant number of the missions we will be called upon to accomplish for which traditional combat effectiveness measures make no sense, we will need to develop new sets of mission measures (e.g., for peacekeeping, a normalcy indicator system might be useful[13]).

Over time, if we make the effort, we will be able to accumulate evidence of the nature of the relationships among key NCW model variables and measures of mission effectiveness for a variety of missions under differing circumstances. From this continuing stream of data, we can establish linkages to value.

Given that we conduct relatively few real experiments, the bulk of this evidence is bound to come from combat models. Unfortunately, most of the models in use today simply do not have the ability to deal with the kinds of changes in command and control, organization, and information flows that make NCW different. Furthermore, most do not adequately represent intelligent, adaptive behavior. These shortcomings, when added to a virtual lack of models that go beyond traditional combat to asymmetric situations or that can represent coalition operations, do not provide us with a good foundation upon which to build. Hence, unless we embark on a serious effort to develop the mission models we need, we will not be able to populate the databases needed to link the NCW model to measures of mission effectiveness.

Models alone, however, are not the answer. No one model can be expected to satisfy the needs of all analyses. There will always be factors that are not represented well in a particular model. Hence, any study team must rely upon a number of models and experimental results, synthesize them, and supplement them with sensitivity analyses. Thus, our ability to establish the links between NCW and value will ultimately depend upon the nature of the empirical analyses and experiments we undertake and upon our ability to conduct high quality analysis.

Transforming DoD Processes to Support Transformation

In any assessment of progress, we need to consider more than just a snapshot of where we are. We have only to look at the adverse consequences of maintaining too great a focus on the next quarter in business to see that we need to measure anticipated future performance in addition to measuring where we are. Thus, the set of transformation measures should contain a set of leading indicators as well as a set of snapshot measures. The "net" as an enabler of NCW is, in effect, a precursor of future NCW capability and thus, is a leading indicator. Progress in our ability to understand NCW is also a leading indicator. Both of these can be directly related to the development of NCW applications. But perhaps the most important influence on our future ability to transform is the state of our business processes.

The current requirements and acquisition processes and their relationships to experimentation are relics of a previous era. The advent of software and its increasing importance in command and control systems brought about a new reality—complex adaptive systems. In 1993, a DoD-Industry Task Force[14] concluded that the basic assumptions that underpin our requirements, acquisition, and PPBS processes were, in fact, incorrect. Specifically, the assumption that we could actually specify requirements (and estimate schedules and costs accurately) before a system was designed and built is simply untenable. One of the main reasons for this is the inability of people to fully understand a new technology and its implications without any experience. Thus, it is impossible to expect that before the system is built (or adequately prototyped) that its requirements can be fully specified. Given the nature of complex adaptive systems, all systems will need to evolve continuously. Hence, development as a phase in a system life cycle cannot be brought to a conclusion. Our PPBS and acquisition processes with their unrealistic desire for an upfront, fixed set of requirements, costs, and schedule and the distinctions they make between development, operations, and maintenance actually contribute to the cost overruns and schedule slippage they are trying to minimize. This DoD-Industry Task Force recommended the use of Evolutionary Acquisition (EA) and associated changes in the PPBS process. Acquisition reform efforts have made progress in giving program managers more flexibility, but progress in acquisition reform has not been enough to keep pace with rapidly advancing information technologies and commercial services. Nor have they begun to address the issue of the acquisition of a mission capability package. Instead, the current acquisition process still focuses on programs.

Bureaucracies are the butts of many a joke. We make fun of their mindlessness and inflexibility. They are the archenemies of change. As such, bureaucracies clearly are obstacles to transformation. Can we create a bureaucracy for change? The problems posed by a set of business practices tuned to the Industrial Age and the Cold War are formidable. The pace of transformation will not only depend upon our ability to generate innovative ideas, but on our ability to bring them to fruition. We need to address the impediments presented by our current approaches to four key processes—requirements, PPBS, acquisition, and experimentation. By identifying the characteristics of these processes that need to change, we can develop measures (or at least indicants) that reflect progress.

Reforms in the requirements process have also taken place, but it is still far too focused on the materiel (the big "M" in DOTMLPF) and not organized and focused around mission capability packages. The relationship between experimentation and requirements determination is currently tenuous at best. Requirements exist and can be specified at different levels. At the mission level, there is currently ample guidance provided by the Defense Planning Guidance. The DPG also provides direction with respect to the nature and focus of the Department's experimentation activities. Experimentation should take over from where the DPG leaves off. Requirements should be a product of experimentation rather than an input to a separate requirements process that adds years to the process and almost guarantees that innovation will take the slowest track to our forces. A transformation of the DoD processes would therefore include:

- **A move from a program-centric approach to a mission capability package approach in our PPBS, acquisition, and requirements processes.** This will provide us with an increased ability to understand in which capabilities we are investing, ascertain their expected value, and more realistically assess progress. It will also provide an improved basis for making program tradeoffs both within and among mission capability packages.

- **Letting the DPG drive experimentation and experimentation drive requirements.** Given the intrinsically joint nature of a network-centric mission capability package, an increased emphasis needs to be placed on joint and coalition experiments at all DoD experimentation venues.

- **Developing a fast track from experimental validation of a mission capability package to the fielding of the mission capability package.** This fast track process should not be an exception to current processes, but should replace current processes as the normal way to do business.

• **Eliminating the distinctions we make between development and O&M for systems, shifting instead to a life cycle model that allocates a certain amount of resources to cover evolution and provide more flexibility to managers.** Managers need to be judged on their ability to get the most out of these resources, not on their ability to hit preconceived (often totally unrealistic) levels of performance and schedules that, in fact, cause dysfunctional behaviors and constrain the ability of systems to adapt.

• **Shifting the focus of our experimentation activities from a preoccupation with mega-events to a balanced approach.** This balanced approach would entail a large number of discovery-oriented events, followed by a smaller number of hypothesis testing experiments, followed by a few demonstrations and prompt adoptions. Currently, there are far too few discovery and hypothesis testing events to adequately support the more visible and well-publicized mega-events.[15]

Metrics that reflect progress in each of these five areas are discussed below.

Measuring Progress Toward a Mission Capability Package Approach

Progress in moving away from a program-centric to a mission capability package approach can be measured by the establishment of a baseline and the use of simple ratios. The baseline consists of all big "M" programs. The sum of the costs of these programs becomes the denominator of the ratio while the costs of the programs that will be accounted for and managed as part of a mission capability package forms the numerator. We should expect this ratio to increase as mission capability packages are formed, accountability is established, and processes are set up to manage these programs.

Measuring Progress To Experiment-Driven Requirements

As we make progress in integrating experimentation into mainstream processes that establish priorities, allocate resources, and shape programs (hopefully collections of activities that are associated with mission capability packages), we can expect to see fewer and fewer requirements documents that are not a direct output of experimentation. Again, a baseline ratio, with the denominator being the number of CRDs and ORDs[16] approved and the numerator reflecting those that were based upon the results of experimentation, should be used.

Measuring Progress in Closing the Gap Between Concept Development and Fielding

There have been a number of initiatives, most notably ACTDs (Advanced Concept and Technology Demonstrations), that are designed to insert new technology into the force on an accelerated basis. However, many ACTDs have not resulted in a deployable product in a timely manner. Furthermore,

ACTDs represent a very small fraction of the investments in technology we make on an annual basis. Thus, even if ACTDs were all very successful and resulted in deployed capabilities in timeframes comparable to industry, the vast majority of our capability would remain on a very slow track.

The bottom line is, of course, the time it takes from the point when we have demonstrated the viability of a concept to its initial operational capability (IOC). We need a valid benchmark of timeliness in order to have a meaningful measure of fast track capability. While industry differs from the DoD in significant ways, an industry benchmark still provides the most meaningful point of comparison we have at this time. Hence, we will need to establish, for different types of capabilities, a corresponding industrial capability to use as a yardstick to measure how well we are doing. Once a benchmark is established, a ratio can be constructed— the denominator being the total number of developments or mission capability packages delivered (IOC) and the numerator being those that accomplished this in a time comparable to industry.

Measuring Progress to a Life Cycle Model

Moving to a true life cycle model will, in all likelihood, require significant changes in traditional ways of thinking and law. Therefore, progress in this area will be manifested in changes in process for some time to come. The DoD needs to develop a long-term strategy to move to a life cycle process that provides flexibility to program (or mission capability package) managers. This plan needs to establish a set of milestones that can be used to measure progress. When progress is sufficient to result in mission capability packages and major programs that have life cycle funding and management processes in place, we will be able to more directly measure progress.

Measuring Progress To Balanced Experimentation

A balanced experimentation program will have a different distribution of activities and expenditures than our current efforts. Obviously, no one knows exactly what this distribution should be.[17] Nevertheless, it is generally agreed that the current distribution is greatly out of balance. Currently, large-scale events dominate the experimentation calendar. A disproportionate amount of time and resources is devoted to just a few events. However, a single 2-week experiment is not sufficient to settle the way a headquarters should be designed. No single experiment can adequately test a particular hypothesis. Given the totality of pressures that are currently being brought to bear on the experimentation community, I think it is unlikely that we will go too far in the near term in allocating more time and resources to discovery and hypothesis experiments instead of the mega-events. Thus, we can measure progress toward a balanced approach to experimentation by the changes in the current distribution, specifically the ratios of the "event days" devoted annually to each of these three kinds of events.

The metrics discussed in this section provide only an initial starting point. However, imperfect as they are, if used, they will give us a better picture than we have today. They will allow us to focus attention on how well we are doing in our efforts to transform the DoD and what areas require more attention. In the process, we will be able to improve these metrics and improve our efforts in transformation.

[1]*Network Centric Warfare Department of Defense Report to Congress*. "Executive Summary." July 2001. p. i.

[2]The definition of agility in terms of these four attributes was developed during an ad hoc U.S./UK meeting to discuss NCW and transformation. Work on the definition of agile command and control is currently in progress.

[3]Alberts, David S. *The Unintended Consequences of Information Age Technologies*. Washington, DC: National Defense University. April 1996. p. 115.

[4]Note that in this report, this is referred to as a "maturity model." Upon further reflection, I believe the term "capability model" is more appropriate.

[5]*Widely* is not meant to imply a disregard for information security.

[6]In fact, the transformation is best viewed as a journey rather than a destination, with each waypoint along the path having value.

[7]*Information Superiority—Making the Joint Vision Happen*. Washington, DC: Department of Defense. 2000. pp.11-12.

[8]A mission organization is the totality of people that are needed to participate in a given mission and the manner in which they are related to one another.

[9]A mission-oriented measure that is easy to understand ultimately gives credibility to a more abstract DoD-level measure.

[10]Alberts, David S. *The Unintended Consequences of Information Age Technologies*. Washington, DC: National Defense University. April 1996. p. 295.

[11]A statistical parameter, the coefficient of variation, reflects the amount of variance explained by a regression (formula that maps the values of a set of independent variables into a value of the dependent variable).

[12]There is a wealth of material regarding measures of mission effectiveness. See: the *NATO COBP for Command and Control Assessment*. Washington, DC: CCRP. 1998.

[13]The *NATO COBP for C2 Assessment* is currently being revised. The revised version, currently in draft form contains a discussion of other mission measures: http://www.dodccrp.org/nato_supp/nato.htm. April 2002.

[14]AFCEA Study Team. *Evolutionary Acquisition Study*. Fairfax, VA: AFCEA. June 7, 1993.

[15]JFCOM Millennium Challenge—http://www.jfcom.mil/About/experiments/mc02.htm. April 2002.

[16]CRDs—capstone requirements documents; ORDs—operational requirements documents.

[17]I will, however, offer the opinion that a better allocation in the number of event days (discovery, hypothesis, mega-demonstration) should be on a ratio of 100–20–1. Given that discovery and hypothesis experiments cost far less per day than a mega-event, we would still be spending the bulk of our experimental dollars on mega-events.

CHAPTER 11

Transformation Roadmap

The development of a DoD Transformation Roadmap is a prerequisite for being able to manage the large set of diverse tasks that need to be undertaken to transform the DoD into an Information Age organization. Work on such a roadmap has recently begun as the Services and Agencies are engaged in the development of their own Transformation Roadmaps.[1] This section addresses the question: "What should a good Transformation Roadmap contain?"

While different people will conjure up different visions when they hear the word *roadmap*, most would agree that a roadmap lays out a path from where we are to where we want to go. In this case, the path is more akin to a critical path[2] than a road. And the destination is not an end, but really a beginning. While Information Age mission capability packages are the most visible and immediate products of a transformation effort and their deployments will surely represent milestones along the way, the transformation of the DoD (the destination) will not be complete until the organization is capable of efficient, timely, and continuous adaptation.

Hence, the set of tasks needed to turn out the first set of network-centric mission capability packages will only form a subset of the network of interrelated tasks that are to be included in a Transformation Roadmap. For as we work on this first set of mission capability packages, we also need to work on the basic processes of the DoD. Thus, a Transformation Roadmap needs to identify not only the tasks directly related to the development of innovations, but also the tasks needed to facilitate innovation, mature concepts, and translate these concepts into real operational capabilities.

Figure 10 depicts the elements of transformation that need to be explicitly addressed in a Transformation Roadmap.

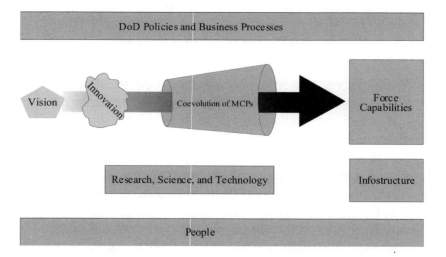

Figure 10. Elements of Transformation

Vision

A Transformation Roadmap should begin with a vision of what the transformed organization would be like. Given that the transformation process is a voyage of discovery, it would be hard to imagine that we could, with any precision, describe what the transformed organization would look like. Hence the vision of the future needs to be expressed in terms of the characteristics that are sought.[3]

The vision provided by the Department's leadership needs to emphasize a determination to harness and leverage information technologies as an essential part of the requirement to maintain the military strength of the United States in the global arena and to protect against asymmetric vulnerabilities arising from foreign exploitation of information technologies. Moreover, this vision should stress the need to tailor systems to missions and to focus attention on mission capability packages as the vehicle for the development and delivery of capabilities in a capabilities-based defense strategy.

Joint Vision 2020, Quadrennial Defense Review, Defense Planning Guidance, Network Centric Warfare Report to Congress, and various Service and Agency documents each offer a perspective on where we want to go. These official policy documents have drawn upon and are augmented by a body of visionary writings by current and former DoD personnel, contractors, and academics. A sense of the future is emerging. The DoD's Transformation Roadmap will be incomplete if it neglects to provide a simple articulation of the nature of a transformed DoD. Given that such a roadmap will be a living document, it should be expected that this articulation would evolve both in content and in its expression.

The vision of DoD transformation provided in a Transformation Roadmap will contribute to developing a broad consensus and understanding of the direction in which our leadership seeks to move. The process of transformation to an Information Age organization needs to be network-centric. It will involve widespread sharing of information and collaboration, and be best accomplished with a management style that seeks to foster self-synchronization. Hence, the roadmap's vision serves as the basis for developing the shared awareness (of the desired future) necessary to achieve the desired emergent behaviors.

Innovation

Following the articulation of the vision, a Transformation Roadmap needs to address how innovation will be fostered. A distinction needs to be made between sustaining and disruptive innovations.[4] Transformation is all about nurturing and maturing disruptive innovations. There should be recognition that current reward and incentive structures and processes favor sustaining innovations at the expense of disruptive ones. The right climate needs to be created for disruptive innovation. Impediments to disruptive innovation need to be removed. The Transformation Roadmap therefore needs to spell out the specific steps that will be taken to foster innovative thinking and protect its producers and products.

Coevolution of Transformational Mission Capability Packages

The Transformation Roadmap needs to identify the initial set of missions for which network-centric mission capability packages will be developed and specify the processes that will be used to coevolve them. Experimentation is central to the coevolution of mission capability packages. A balanced experimentation program of discovery, hypothesis testing, and demonstration events needs to be laid out as part of a campaign. The campaign must be designed to take innovative ideas for accomplishing missions, test and refine them, demonstrate their value, and finally develop deployable capabilities. Research, experimentation, and demonstration processes are not sufficiently well-coupled to the processes that acquire and field operational capabilities.

Infostructure

Achieving a transformed force depends upon putting in place a robust, secure, and interoperable network, populating it with quality information and services, and protecting it. The Transformation Roadmap needs to contain a plan to migrate our legacy capabilities to this vision of an integrated infostructure. Furthermore, as indicated elsewhere in this book, current ideas about information dissemination and "information management" need to be replaced with newer notions. Systems and processes that rely on push need to be reoriented to rely on pull. A post-before-use paradigm needs to replace the current sense of information ownership. The Transformation Roadmap also needs to address how these changes in philosophy and approach will be incorporated into system design and acquisition activities.

Investment Strategy

Naturally, a roadmap would not be very useful if it did not contain an investment strategy that provided the details of how resources will be allocated (or reallocated) to achieve the desired results. Requirements drive (or should drive) investment priorities by allowing us to identify the deltas between where we are and where we want to go. For example, we already possess a great deal of equipment and a large number of systems. NCW requires that we have a robustly networked force. It follows that we should place a high priority on making the battlespace entities we have "net ready" and building out the infostructure necessary to provide the links and the information services needed (e.g., collaborative environments). It also stands to reason that we take the necessary steps to ensure that we secure our network and information.

But we will not be able to do this in a year or even in the Five-Year Defense Program. Priorities need to be established and related to achieving time-phased capabilities. A roadmap needs to clearly illuminate the migration strategy chosen, identifying the phases involved in making the network robust and connecting battlespace entities to it. A strategy based upon selected mission capability packages and the network improvements, the platform retrofits, and the new capabilities needed to make these mission capability packages operational will increase the chances that investments will be coordinated and focused.

Warfighters can and should help shape the requirements for information and networks and influence the DoD's investments in these by playing an active role in the mission capability package coevolution process. The technical and operational communities need to work much more closely together to develop new mission capability package concepts and to refine these concepts. Given the institutional inertia involved in some components of a mission capability package, these concepts need to be incubated and nurtured long before the technology reaches the marketplace. Defense planners and budgeters need to think more in terms of mission capability packages than in terms of individual programs, using mission capability packages to link the programmatic activities needed to implement or maintain a mission capability package. This would help ensure that all of the necessary components are adequately funded and properly synchronized, thus eliminating one significant cause for a mission capability package's lack of completeness or coherence.

Research, Science, and Technology

Private sector efforts, particularly in Information Age technologies, will surely drive what products and information services will be available in the future. The DoD conducts and sponsors a great deal of research to explore areas that are not expected to be adequately addressed by private sector R&D. Nevertheless, some avenues of research central to DoD Transformation are not receiving adequate attention either in the DoD or the private sector. The DoD Transformation

Roadmap needs to identify these key areas and contain a plan for addressing them. Included should be increased attention to military sensemaking (at the individual, team, distributed team, organizational, and societal levels), command and control approaches that can effectively shape the behavior of complex adaptive systems, techniques and technologies that effectively deal with variations in perception, and a variety of topics related to the integration and testing of federations of heterogeneous systems. These are discussed in more detail in Chapter 13, Research.

Another area of weakness is our ability to represent (model) and analyze key NCW concepts and relationships. Given the empirical imperative of such research, the relationship between research, modeling, analysis activities, and experimentation needs to be explicitly addressed.

People

However often it is said that people are our most valuable asset, it is not said often enough.[5] An Information Age transformation of the DoD requires a workforce that has been properly educated, trained, motivated, rewarded, and empowered. Our people will need the right sets of skills and experiences. No Transformation Roadmap would be complete without attention to acquiring and retaining the skills, expertise, and experience needed in an Information Age organization. No Transformation Roadmap would be complete without addressing the steps that will be taken to provide a stimulating and rewarding environment for our people.

DoD Policies and Business Processes

It merits repeating. Current DoD policies and processes create major impediments to progress. If success depends upon our ability to coevolve mission capability packages, then it stands to reason that we need to manage progress, not by function or program, but by mission capabilities. Our planning and budgeting processes need to be organized around mission capabilities. Oversight and management need to "matrix" with the primary focus not on collections of similar programs, but on mission capability packages. Only then will we be able to put the needed resources, performance, and schedule tradeoffs in their proper context. In addition to developing friendly mission capability package planning, budgeting, and acquisition processes, these network-centric, inherently joint mission capability packages need a secure, robust, and interoperable infostructure, much of which will consist of COTS technology and shrink-wrapped software. The collection of systems we have today will not meld into a coherent infostructure without a great deal of attention and effort. Making this happen will require changes in processes and behaviors that serve to put the needs of enterprise first and local organizations second in decisions regarding the design and acquisition of the disparate pieces that collectively form the infostructure. There are serious discussions underway in each of the Services and Agencies about changes that would make it easier for them to provide the infostructure that they need and to coevolve mission capability packages. A Transformation Roadmap would not be complete without addressing the nature of the changes needed to remove or significantly reduce the existing impediments to progress.

Navigation Aids for the Transformation Journey

A roadmap needs to be able to give a sense of where we are relative to where we came from and where we want to go. If we stray off course, a roadmap should show it. Thus, a roadmap needs to have a locator system and milestones that represent progress.

---

[1]*Quadrennial Defense Review Report.* Washington, DC: Department of Defense. September 30, 2001. http://www.defenselink.mil/pubs/qdr2001.pdf.

[2]The critical path is "the longest path through the network in terms of the total duration of tasks." http://www-2.cs.cmu.edu/~ornar/MSD/slides/pert.ppt. April 2002.

[3]That is why the tenets of NCW are framed as they are, not in terms of what a NCW solution looks like, but in terms of the characteristics (e.g., shared awareness) that it possesses.

[4]*Network Centric Warfare Department of Defense Report to Congress.* July 2001. pp. 5-1 to 5-12.

[5]The Secretary of Defense has developed a set of 13 principles for the DoD. Number 3 says, in part, "Nothing is more important than the men and women who work in this Department—they are its heart and soul and its future." Memorandum dated February 27, 2002.

CHAPTER 12

The Way Ahead

A long with the development of a Transformation Roadmap, attention needs to be paid to the way we think about doctrine, education, training, and the way we approach test and evaluation.

Doctrine

Historically, doctrine has been a distillation of best practice and lessons learned, which over time were clearly documented to form the basis for the initiation of new recruits. It is predicated on the fact that there is a best way to do things and that we know what that best way is. Today we are in a period of transition. The old ways of doing business are in the process of being replaced with new ways. This would not necessitate a fundamental change in the process of doctrine creation if it were not for the fact that the dynamics of change are such that we will forevermore be in a transition. That is, change will not be episodic, but continual. A new way of doing business will not remain the best way for very long. Thus, the entire notion of doctrine needs to be changed from one of publishing "the way" it should be done to a dynamic process of learning and sharing best practice.

The various doctrine communities should be involved at the beginning of the mission capability package concept development process and stay involved throughout this process. In NCW, one should not make distinctions between joint and Service doctrine, for doing so contributes to the probability that there will be disconnects and conflicts that will adversely affect mission performance. Only by making NCW precepts the foundation of all doctrine can we ensure that information will be properly shared, appropriate collaborations will take place, and that forces can self-synchronize.

Traditional doctrine is currently an obstacle to progress. Organizations and individuals feel bound to honor it and thus create a mindset and environment not conducive to disruptive innovation. This is because when the nature and distribution of information changes, radical new ways of doing business and complications in the old ways of doing business emerge. In many cases, new or modified doctrine can ease newly created frictions or simplify the changes necessary to adapt. Changes in doctrine are often essential if the benefits of new information systems are to be realized and inconsistencies between capacity and doctrine avoided. Doctrine should be viewed as fluid and helpful, not static and restrictive.

Involving the doctrine community early will also facilitate the key process of embedding doctrine in new systems. It should be recognized that doctrine is being written or changed when decisions are made about who can receive some class of information, who has the workstations from which a database can be updated, or who is able to access and use some classes of data. This process needs to be consciously and carefully monitored. Unless the doctrine community is involved, technical personnel responding to technical criteria and standards will be, in effect, making doctrine by default. If, however, the doctrine community is involved, new systems being fielded will contain and help support the evolution of doctrine.

Education and Training

Professional Military Education (PME) must serve as a change agent for the military grappling with the Information Age. Raising awareness of the threat, opportunities, and vulnerabilities inherent in the changes underway can best be done through the PME structure. A "teaching hospital" model should be adopted so that this new information is conveyed in the context of real-world experience and actions, and its impact can be direct and effective.

While some progress has been made toward bringing PME into the Information Age, the process needs to be accelerated. This involves significant changes in the curriculum so that all students (not just the ones that are in technical specialties) become current in information technologies (including their advantages, vulnerabilities, limits, and applications) and familiar with their likely impact on military affairs. PME institutions need to develop methods of teaching that enable (and require) students to become computer literate and knowledgeable of how to obtain information electronically. Connectivity within and among PME institutions should be routine as well as connectivity between PME institutions and the DoD and industry simulation and training centers with which they have natural synergy.

Training is perhaps the arena of military affairs where information technology has already had its most profound effect, but also remains an arena where much more can and should be done. While educated military professionals are already trained on specific information systems, these systems must be mastered and their practical limits learned in the more realistic training environments. In addition, the emphasis needs to shift from a focus on individual systems to a focus on the network. Moreover, improvements in virtual reality technologies and connectivity are needed to provide options for diverse mission rehearsal and training at a fraction of the cost of field exercises. Defining when and where these lower cost training opportunities exist and taking advantage of them must remain a priority. The most cost-effective systems will be those that possess embedded training packages and provide near real-time feedback, easing the comprehension and retention of lessons learned.

Test and Evaluation

The transformation strategy described in this book will result in significant changes in the way we will employ, acquire, and field systems. These changes pose significant challenges for the test and evaluation community.[1]

NCW involves a historic shift in the center of gravity from platforms to the network. In NCW, the single greatest contributor to combat power is the network itself. The value of platforms, headquarters, and other assets derive their value (in NCW) from their ability to contribute to the overall effort by virtue of their being connected to the net. The marginal value of an unconnected platform pales in comparison to the value it can generate if it is networked. For example, the information generated by a networked sensor serves to enhance the value of all of the other nodes on the net rather than only a few nodes. Given this shift in value, the focus of test and evaluation needs to shift from a focus on the performance of individual battlespace entities to their ability to add to the value of the networked force.

The ASD(C3I) (who is dually hatted as the Department's CIO) is working to provide the infostructure needed to support network-centric operations and the transformation of DoD business processes.[2] His organization is committed to:

- Making information available on a network that people depend on and trust;

- Populating the network with new, dynamic sources of information to defeat the enemy; and

- Denying the enemy information advantages and exploiting their weaknesses.

Toward these ends, the OASD(C3I) is working to deploy a ubiquitous, secure, and robust network eliminating bandwidth, frequency, and computing capacity limitations. To enhance their ability to make sense out of the available information, they are working to deploy collaborative environments and other performance support tools. At the same time, they are working to ensure that the DoD network and its information is secure and assured.

Network Centric Warfare is about the sharing of information. This will require policies and programs that ensure that the net is populated and continuously refreshed with quality data including intelligence, nonintelligence, raw, and processed. Information not on the net has very limited value. It is recognized that all users of information are also suppliers and that as suppliers they have a responsibility to post information before they use it, thereby ensuring that all the information is available to those who need it. This move away from a "supplier push" mentality is simply a recognition of the fact that no one can possibly know everyone who can put the information to good use, appreciate the tolerance for ambiguity of others, or understand how the information could be effectively used. A move from push to pull shifts the burden for finding the information they need to the users.

Awareness, a touchstone of NCW, is not a property of a system but an attribute to be found in the cognitive domain. Measuring what information is available in a system is not an adequate measure of the level of awareness achieved. We would be remiss if we did not address the myriad issues related to the ability of our forces to make sense out of the information available on the net.

Information is not always easy to get. Our ability to populate the net with quality information will depend, in part, upon our ability to develop new ways to gain access to information. We seek to surprise the enemy with the information we are using by collecting persistent, responsive, exquisite intelligence. An important aspect of the transformation involves a shift in the nature of the missions we are able to perform. For the most part, these nontraditional missions require new types of information that, in turn, involve new sources.

At the same time that we are enhancing our own information-related capabilities, we must seek to deny these advantages to others. Therefore, our ability to conduct offensive information operations is essential. As adversaries will seek to do the same to us, we must implement full spectrum security.

It is clear that the properties that we seek to achieve are not properties of a system but properties of a network, a network that is dynamic in a number of dimensions. It is also clear that the DoD's efforts cannot be confined to the physical and information domains, but need to extend to the cognitive domain. We must move beyond the current focus of supporting individual commanders or units to a broader focus of supporting groups of distributed individuals working collaboratively.

The challenges for both the development and T&E communities are considerable. New ways to instrument, analyze, and evaluate federations of systems and distributed teams operating in a networked environment are needed. Reality is the only "test environment" that will allow us to adequately test new systems along with coevolved processes. We will therefore need to find ways to add and subtract systems and capabilities to the current baseline, without destroying the integrity/security of the operational system, assessing proposed increments both *in situ* and on the fly. Perhaps our greatest challenge will be to assess our ability to deal with various types of attacks on our system while ensuring that vital operations are not harmed or degraded.

We also need measures that reflect more than system performance or indeed the performance of a federation of systems. We need to be able to assess all of the links in the NCW value chain. But the transformation of test and evaluation will be about more than what is measured and how it is measured, it will also be about how test and evaluation activities relate to the organizations and processes that develop new concepts and coevolve mission capability packages. Central to this coevolution process is experimentation. One cannot say in advance exactly what level of performance is needed, nor the consequences associated with higher or lower levels of performance. Hence, it makes no sense to try to establish pass/fail standards in advance. In fact, it is just these things that concept-based experimentation is supposed to determine. The partnership between developers and operators that is developing in experimentation settings needs to extend to the test and evaluation community as well. We need to work toward achieving a process in which all the participants lend their expertise and experience to first innovate, and then refine and improve a capability over time.

There is an imperfect yet telling analogy that can be drawn involving the changes that have taken place in the business world between producers and suppliers. Once there existed an arm's length, almost adversarial, relationship between producers and suppliers. Neither would share information with the other for fear that it would be used against them. Today you see producers and suppliers working closely together to achieve greater levels of quality and efficiency. Suppliers now have a much better idea of what the needs of producers are, and producers now better understand what it takes to supply them with what they need. The net result has been greater stability, dramatic improvements in cost structures, and higher quality, resulting in improved value to customers and more profit all around. A closer working relationship between T&E and the operational and technical communities promises analogous gains.

What We Need to Measure

Network Centric Warfare is predicated upon the ability to create and share a high level of awareness and to use this shared awareness to rapidly self-synchronize effects. This will allow us to bring all the available information and all of our assets to bear, greatly increasing combat power. Of course, NCW requires that we think about information differently, particularly the way we disseminate it. Peer-to-peer relationships and information exchanges will predominate. The edge of the organization will be empowered. Command will often involve choosing from a set of alternatives presented from the edge, rather than guiding a centralized planning process. This in turn affects the attributes of information systems that are most important to us and hence has profound implications for test and evaluation.

The T&E community has a lot to offer, but its contribution to the transformation will depend upon its own transformation. An independent, highly professional test and evaluation community is needed more than ever to ensure that the capabilities being developed and deployed are thoroughly tested and accurately assessed. It will, however, take a concerted effort for the operational, experimentation, and various test and evaluation communities to come together to achieve this goal.

---

[1]This section is based upon a draft of a guest editorial by-line John Stenbit, the ASD(C3I), prepared for the *ITEA Journal*'s June issue.

[2]For a discussion of the ASD(C3I)'s vision and priorities, see www.c3i.osd.mil.

CHAPTER 13

Research

To support the transformation of the DoD, more research is needed in at least the following six specific areas:

1. Performance characteristics of federations of Information Age systems;

2. Cognitive processes;

3. Behaviors of distributed teams;

4. Collaboration;

5. Sensemaking; and

6. New command concepts.

Performance Characteristics of Federations of Information Age Systems

The systems environment in which we will operate in the Information Age will differ in a number of significant ways from the systems environment we became accustomed to in the last decades of the 20th century. A major assumption that is at the heart of traditional approaches to modeling is that we can understand the complexity of our systems by decomposing them and getting a handle on the pieces. This bottom-up approach was never able to keep up with the growing complexity of the systems we were building, nor the increasing lack of control we could exercise over the behavior of the collection of systems we use. A brute force approach, one based upon identifying all of the threads through a system and systematically testing each one, quickly becomes intractable by virtue of the fact that the performance of the system as a whole is dependent on the distribution of active threads. Hence, they could not be tested in isolation. The combinatorial challenge simply proved too great. We currently lack the science and technology for building networks that behave like complex adaptive systems. Therefore, a new approach to understanding the dynamics of complex systems behavior (the ecology of systems) is needed to help us understand and predict performance in all of the dimensions of interest. Included among these dimensions are system response times, availability, repeatability, security, and performance under stresses of various kinds. These stresses can be a result of nonmalicious degradations caused by the dynamics of the battlefield and disruptions caused by component and/or communications failures. But they can also be caused by deliberate, orchestrated, malicious acts of an adversary. The basics of system engineering (design, protocols, and approaches to hardware and software development and testing) need to be reviewed and new approaches better suited to federated systems in a hostile environment need to be developed. New models that reflect the reality of federations of systems and a hostile environment need to be developed as well so that we can do a better job of predicting infostructure performance (system scalability), identifying and understanding our vulnerabilities, developing better methods to recognize and manage anomalies and their consequences, and developing strategies to deny adversaries the use of effective information systems.

In addition to developing an ability to understand the behavior of complex adaptive systems, we need to develop better approaches to engineering federations of systems. There will always be a crippling legacy problem if we do not develop new approaches to scalable "plug and play" approaches that involve dynamically negotiated protocols that give a collection of systems the ability to accept new players and to migrate itself to newer and better protocols. A number of "end to end" capabilities need to emerge from a collection of systems for the collection to be useful in military operations. These "end to end" properties include assured delivery, authentication, security, and interoperability (both technical and semantic).

A shift from information push to information pull is necessary to achieve the level of information sharing needed to support NCW. How this shift will affect the federation of systems is not clear. We need theories and models that help us understand the implications of this shift and to predict behaviors. We also need to develop the "announcements,"[1] browsers, and agents needed to recognize new sources of information as they emerge and incorporate them into anticipatory pull arrangements.

The DoD requires collaboration environments that adequately support the full range of collaborative behaviors needed for NCW. The ability to support many independent groups simultaneously puts an enormous stress on a federation of systems. As if on cue, the concepts and technologies that constitute what is known as Internet 3.0[2] are beginning to emerge from corporate R&D into the marketplace. The implications of these technologies, and the way in which they are likely to develop, need to be better understood.

Cognitive Processes

Higher levels of NCW maturity rely heavily upon the achievement of shared awareness. Awareness is not a system property of a human-machine interfacing, but a property of human cognition. Among the determinants of the level of awareness achieved and the degree to which it is shared are perceptions, a priori knowledge, familiarity with the situation, the mix of information and misinformation present, the order in which information is received, and trust relationships. The degree to which awareness is shared depends upon many of these same factors as well as differences among the team members in knowledge, skills, experience, and culture. How these all play together is an area that we do not sufficiently understand. Answering questions related to how cognitive processes and the independent variables that influence these processes affect awareness and shared awareness in military situations needs to be a top research priority.

Humans have trouble in dealing with uncertainty and risk. Yet uncertainty and risk are an inherent part of military operations. We need to focus some research on these areas so that we can better understand not only how to improve an individual's ability to deal with them, but to understand how differences that exist from individual to individual affect their interactions.

Behaviors of Distributed Teams

As NCW becomes a reality, more of the tasks that militaries undertake will be performed by distributed teams. How teams work is a subject that has received some attention, but little of it has been focused in military domains with the pressures inherent in these situations. The interactions that have been possible have, of course been limited to the capabilities of our information and telecommunications systems. The enormous improvements in the "richness of interaction" (the third dimension, after richness and reach, of the economics of information) that are in the pipeline are sure to affect the behavior of distributed teams. We need to know far more than we currently do about this behavior so that we can better focus our experiments and determine the ranges of expected team performance.

Collaboration

Collaboration is also a key component of mature applications of NCW principles. Collaborative processes in military organizations, particularly collaboration across echelons and horizontal functional collaboration, are relatively new and untested. There is a limited body of knowledge in this area—a body of knowledge that needs to be significantly expanded and applied to the military domain. Work needs to be done to identify the various forms of collaboration, understand their characteristics, and relate them to military tasks and situations. Coalitions will be of particular importance in future military operations. Cross-cultural collaborations present a unique set of challenges that must be better understood.

Sensemaking

Our current view of military decisionmaking is far too simplistic. Recent research has demonstrated that the rational decisionmaking process taught in many business schools is not the one that is actually used by experts in highly stressful situations. The deliberate planning process used by military headquarters is currently based upon the rational model of option generation and evaluation. Research in both U.S. Marine Corps and U.S. Army command centers has shown that the deliberate course of action and planning processes are seldom used. The dominant alternative, naturalistic decisionmaking, depends on the commander or decisionmaker perceiving the situation as "familiar" or within their expertise. When this condition does not apply, they are likely to first seek a dominant course of action (one they perceive will be successful regardless of what the adversary does or how the situation develops). Failing to find a dominant course of action, military decisionmakers can be expected to apply a "minimax" approach, seeking to minimize the likelihood of an undesirable outcome first, then seeking to maximize their own expected utility within the remaining decision space. Only when all these approaches fail will commanders apply the formal logic of multi-attribute utility theory (MAUT) that underlies deliberate course of action analysis and planning. This process may not be the best way to make sense out of a situation. A review of past failures[3] indicates that the errors that were made were a result, not of a lack of the proper information, but of the inability to make sense out of it. Sensemaking encompasses the range of cognitive activities undertaken by individuals, teams, organizations, and indeed societies to develop awareness and understanding and to relate this understanding to a feasible action space. A major research effort is needed to explore the issues in sensemaking, the factors that influence our sensemaking abilities, and how it relates to military situations, both familiar and unfamiliar.

The improvement of sensemaking[4] within a network-centric organizational construct requires an understanding of individual and collective processes by which tacit knowledge (e.g., experience, expertise, culture) is combined with real-time information to identify, form, and articulate appropriate decision points in an ongoing military operation. These processes can be described in terms of four general capabilities involved in the transformation of real-time battlespace information into appropriate decision events and command intent:

1. Shared Situation Awareness—the capability to extract meaningful activities and patterns from the battlespace picture and to share this awareness across the network with appropriate participants.

2. Congruent Understanding and Prediction—the capability to temporally project these activities and patterns into alternative futures so as to identify emerging opportunities and threats.

3. Effective Decisionmaking—the capability to form focused and timely decisions that proactively and accurately respond to these

emerging opportunities and threats with available means and capabilities.

4. Clear and Consistent Command Intent—the capability to articulate decisions in terms of desired goals/effects, constraints, and priorities that are functionally aligned across the network and with other participating organizations.

Sensemaking extends from the cognitive domain into the information domain inasmuch as it is built upon a real-time battlespace picture created by the fusion and display of data and information from a variety of electronic and human sources available to the network.

Sensemaking also relies upon hardware/software capabilities within the information domain to support collaboration and synchronization through the exchange of information, issues, perspectives, and command intent among network participants. As such, research within the fields of computer science, information science, and cognitive science is needed to make meaningful contributions to an understanding of individual and organizational sensemaking through improved visualization methods, decision support tools, and collaboration support tools. As part of this, research should also focus on the degree to which existing information system technology represents an obstacle to maintaining organizational agility and sensemaking reliability under conditions of high stress and situational novelty.

However, the bulk of sensemaking performance at the individual, team, and organization levels falls largely within the cognitive domain. Sensemaking in military operations involves streams of decision events that occur simultaneously over different functional areas. Here, it is expected that the fields of cognitive psychology, group/team dynamics, organizational psychology, management science, sociology, political science, history, and complexity theory will make substantial contributions in addressing the following clusters of research issues:

Structural Issues—How is tacit knowledge formed, organized, shared, reconciled, and used within the organization? What are the specific knowledge structures most often used in capturing military experience, expertise, and culture within an organization (e.g., idioms, paradigms, theories of action, third-order controls, stories)? How commonly held are these structures and what are the mechanisms for identifying and reconciling important differences? To what degree can these structures be explicitly captured and documented in the form of goals, effects, constraints, templates, procedures, and policy? How is tacit knowledge distributed within an organization in comparison to the availability of real-time information? How is tacit knowledge aligned or misaligned with decision authority within an organization? To what degree can tacit knowledge be explicitly codified and made available through training for improving the cohesiveness of command and staff operations?

Process Issues—How are these various knowledge structures employed to reduce situational ambiguity or to cope with information overload? In what ways can the sensemaking process collapse through the emergence of nonlinearity or novelty? How do individuals and expert teams exchange and reconcile tacit knowledge differences across different domains of expertise? How does leadership style affect the management of the sensemaking process within the organization? In what ways are windows of decision opportunity identified and formed (e.g., decision parameters, constraints, objectives) within an ongoing operation? What conditions dictate the use of a particular decision modality (e.g., formal analytic, recognition primed, risk management)? How do individuals, teams, and organizations cope with streams of simultaneous decision windows (i.e., avoid attention fixation, misuse of expertise, etc)?

Adjustment Issues—How do individuals and teams rapidly acquire new tacit knowledge in novel situations where previous experience, expertise, and culture are no longer relevant? As organizations face complex and novel operational environments, what are the various structural, cognitive, and procedural mechanisms for adjusting the sensemaking process and maintaining decisionmaking reliability? In what ways do fixed organizational structures, procedures, and authority patterns present obstacles to maintaining organizational agility and reliability under conditions of high stress and environmental novelty?

A major research effort is needed to address these issues. Given the important influence of cultural differences on the effectiveness of sensemaking activities, this research needs to be conducted not only from a joint perspective, but also from a coalition one as well.

New Command Concepts

Most of what we call command and control research is focused upon the technologies and systems that support command and control. Some is focused upon staff processes. Almost no research is focused on the nature of command and control itself. NCW, in its most mature form, involves profound changes in the role of a commander and the relationships between a commander, a commander's staff, subordinates, and superiors. NCW impacts who has what information, how well the situation is understood, and the degree to which this understanding is shared. As a result, the information environment in which our forces will operate differs considerably from the information environment that prevailed when our current approach to command and control was developed. It took a very long time for our current notions about command and control to evolve. We can not afford the time it will take to naturally adapt to changes in the information environment.

Although we have some experiences with new organizational forms and management approaches in other domains, we have only limited experience and a very limited amount of experimentation data regarding the effectiveness of new approaches to command and control. What we have is promising, but not nearly enough to understand how best to exercise command and control in this new information environment.

Therefore, we need to undertake a major research effort to understand the command and control implications of an Information Age environment. We need to test and verify the tenets of NCW. For example, we need to find answers to the following questions. Under what circumstances does self-synchronization work? How can command intent be best articulated? What sorts of command interventions are needed to maintain control?

Coalition command and control is an area that merits special attention. Experience with coalition operations over the last decade shows that our preconceived notions of how this should work do not pan out in practice. Instead of having one objective function to maximize, as in the case where someone is clearly in charge, coalition operations involve multiple objective functions in a state of tension. This research is needed to help focus and guide our growing experimentation activities. A small amount of well-directed research will result in a far more effective and efficient program of experimentation, paying for itself in short order.

In fact, I think that the time has come to reconsider the use of the term "command and control," particularly in the coalition context. Any reconsideration of Industrial Age command and control is bound to make many commanders uncomfortable. However, consideration of new command concepts is an inherent part of the transformation to an Information Age organization. "Command" implies that there is someone in charge. In a coalition environment (in fact it could be argued, in most circumstances), no single entity is in charge. Rather, the goals of an operation are derived from a consultative process. The same is true when it comes to carrying out intent. No one entity is in charge. Progress is made by virtue of a series of collaborations. Finally, the very notion of control is hard to reconcile with the complexity of today's environments and operations. Convergence seems like a more realistic goal. Hence, I would think that C3 should now stand for Consultation, Collaboration, and Convergence. At any rate, a research effort in this area will eventually show us the limits of command and control, or if you will, C3.

---

[1]Announcements are needed to let the users (pullers) of information aware of the new source.

[2]Fagin, Robert and Chris Kwak. *Internet Infrastructure and Services*. Bear Stearns. May 2001.

[3]The *CCRP Sensemaking Report*—http://www.dodccrp.org/ Sm_Symposium/docs/FinalReport/Sensemaking_Final_Report.htm. April 2002.

[4]This discussion of sensemaking borrows heavily upon conversations with and material prepared by Dr. Richard Hayes and Dr. Dennis Leedom of Evidence Based Research, Inc.

CHAPTER 14

Concluding Thoughts

U nintended consequences will naturally accompany the introduction of Information Age concepts and technologies as individuals and organizations adapt their behaviors and processes. Some of these unintended consequences will, if not properly recognized and managed, cause significant problems that could affect the success of military operations. Other unintended consequences, if properly recognized, offer opportunities for dramatic increases in military effectiveness and efficiency. Thus, there is potential for both the benefits as well as the dangers. By working to create the proper environment to foster innovation and by adopting an approach to change based upon the coevolution of mission capability packages, the risks can be effectively managed while we increase the probability that opportunities will be recognized and seized.

Recent experiences in Afghanistan have shown that we have certainly not lost our ability to innovate under fire. We must all work hard to make this spirit of innovation not a wartime-only event, but part and parcel of everyday life.

1994 - Present

Title	Author(s)	Year
COMMAND AND CONTROL		
Coalition Command and Control	Maurer	1994
Command, Control, and the Common Defense	Allard	1996
Command and Control in Peace Operations	Alberts & Hayes	1995
Command Arrangements for Peace Operations	Alberts & Hayes	1995
Complexity, Global Politics, and National Security	Alberts & Czerwinski	1997
Coping with the Bounds	Czerwinski	1998
INFORMATION TECHNOLOGIES AND INFORMATION WARFARE		
Behind the Wizard's Curtain	Krygiel	1999
Defending Cyberspace and Other Metaphors	Libicki	1997
Defensive Information Warfare	Alberts	1996
Dominant Battlespace Knowledge	Johnson & Libicki	1996
From Network-Centric to Effects-Based Operations	Smith	2002
Information Age Anthology Vol. I	Alberts & Papp	1997
Information Age Anthology Vol. II	Alberts & Papp	2000
Information Age Anthology Vol. III	Alberts & Papp	2001
Information Age Transformation	Alberts	2002
Understanding Information Age Warfare	Alberts, Garstka, Hayes, & Signori	2001
Information Warfare and International Law	Greenberg, Goodman, & Soo Hoo	1998
The Mesh and the Net	Libicki	1994
Network Centric Warfare	Alberts, Garstka, & Stein	1999
Standards: The Rough Road to the Common Byte	Libicki	1995
The Unintended Consequences of Information Age Technologies	Alberts	1996
What Is Information Warfare?	Libicki	1995
OPERATIONS OTHER THAN WAR		
Confrontation Analysis: How to Win Operations Other Than War	Howard	1999
Doing Windows	B. Hayes & Sands	1999
Humanitarian Assistance and Disaster Relief in the Next Century	Sovereign	1998
Information Campaigns for Peace Operations	Avruch, Narel, & Siegel	2000
Interagency and Political-Military Dimensions of Peace Operations: Haiti	Daly Hayes & Wheatley, eds.	1996
Lessons from Bosnia: The IFOR Experience	Wentz, ed.	1998
Lessons from Kosovo: The KFOR Experience	Wentz, ed.	2002
NGOs and the Military in the Interagency Process	Davidson, Landon, & Daly Hayes	1996
Operations Other Than War	Alberts & Hayes	1995
Shock and Awe: Achieving Rapid Dominance	Ullman & Wade	1996
Target Bosnia: Integrating Information Activities in Peace Operations	Siegel	1998

For further information on CCRP, please visit our Web site at

www.dodccrp.org

Order Form

Title_____ Name_____ e-mail_____
Company_____
Address_____
City_____State____ Zip_____ Country_____

A fax cover sheet has been provided for your convenience on the reverse side of this form.

ALLOW 4 TO 6 WEEKS FOR DELIVERY

Quantity	Titles in Stock	CCRP Use Only
	Behind the Wizard's Curtain	95015
	Command Arrangements for Peace Operations	95743
	Command, Control, and the Common Defense	D4699
	Complexity, Global Politics, and National Security	D4946
	Confrontation Analysis	723-125
	Doing Windows	D4698
	Dominant Battlespace Knowledge	95743D
	Humanitarian Assistance and Disaster Relief in the Next Century	D6192
	Information Age Anthology Vol. I	FY0103
	Information Age Anthology Vol. II	D9727
	Information Age Anthology Vol. III	FY0102
	Information Age Transformation	
	Information Campaigns for Peace Operations	518-843
	Interagency and Political-Military Dimensions of Peace Operations: Haiti	95743C
	The Mesh and the Net	93339A
	Network Centric Warfare	518-270
	Standards: The Rough Road to the Common Byte	93339B
	Understanding Information Age Warfare	D5297
	2000 CCRTS CD-ROM	CD00
	4th Int'l CCRTS CD-ROM	CD4I
	5th Int'l CCRTS CD-ROM	CD5I
	2002 CCRTS CD-ROM	CD02

Order # _____
CCRP Use Only

FAX COVER SHEET

CCRP publications are available at no cost through DoD. Complete the order form on the reverse side and fax the sheets or mail to c/o address below.

To: Publications Coordinator
Fax: (703) 821-7742
E-mail: ccrp_pubs@ebrinc.com

From:
Telephone:
Fax:
E-mail:
Date:
Pages: 02

Additional Information:

c/o EBR, Inc. ♦ 1595 Spring Hill RD ♦ Suite 250 ♦ Vienna, VA 22182-2216